Growing Gills

Also by Jessica Abel

Out on the Wire: The Storytelling Secrets of the New Masters of Radio
Trish Trash: Rollergirl of Mars
La Perdida
Mirror, Window
Soundtrack

By Jessica Abel and Matt Madden

Drawing Words & Writing Pictures
Mastering Comics

Growing Gills

How to Find Creative Focus
When You're Drowning in Your Daily Life

Jessica Abel

Published by Jessica Abel.
Jessicaabel.com
ISBN: 9781521277874

Editor: Mikola DeRoo
Designer: Natalie McGuire
Copyeditor: Louise Kennedy
Cover and interior illustrations by Jessica Abel except where noted.
Author photo by Laurène DuCrocq

Acknowledgements:
My deep appreciation goes to Mika, Louise, Natalie, and Jen for their help in editing and producing this book. I could not have pulled this off without them. I would also like to thank Matt, Donna, Natasha, Breanne, and Tara for their support and inspiration, as well as Thomas Marsh and Kevin Haworth for their editorial help and encouragement.
Special thanks go to the Growing Gills Launch Team, the best street team a body could ask for!

First edition, May, 2017.

To my students in the Creative Focus Workshop.

Your dedication to your creative practice,
despite all the obstacles life throws in your way,
is a daily inspiration.

Table of Contents

PART 3: ALIGNING YOUR TODAY WITH YOUR TOMORROW 141

PART 4: FALLING DOWN & GETTING UP 215

CONCLUSION: DESIGNING A SUSTAINING CREATIVE PRACTICE TAKES TIME, SO GO EASY ON YOURSELF   243

Introduction

It's Not Unusual

When I got started on this book, I was teaching an intensive master seminar on storytelling. My group had spent almost three weeks diving generously into each other's work, picking it apart with the utmost care and sensitivity, helping each author weave together threads that could seem impossibly tangled. The workshop participants were amazingly accomplished, fascinating creators of comics, prose books, academic work, and poetry, each with ambitious, compelling stories to tell.

We'd talked about each of their stories a number of times, and so in the last day or two of the workshop, I asked them for feedback on my proposal for this book. I felt a little weird about it because I was supposed to be the teacher, and I didn't want to steal precious class time for my project. But they were eager to help.

The response to the very first line of the proposal surprised me. Addressing the imagined reader of *Growing Gills*, I had written, "You've got a big, gorgeous idea you're incubating that you're struggling to make real." This opening seemed like a pretty safe assumption. After all, who picks up a book about building creative work into their lives not having decided to make something?

But then Liz, an explosively creative, imaginative novelist-in-the-making, told me, "Having a big gorgeous idea is not something...reading the opening line of this, I would self-select out immediately. I'm not at that point. I've felt like a bunch of mashed potatoes." She was almost in tears.

"I spent months in preparation for this workshop, just to have an idea," Liz confessed. "I almost emailed you a couple of times just to ask, 'What should I do to prepare?' Because I felt so, so lost."

She self-selected out. Liz thought she had "no ideas," and even if she managed to let a few squeeze through, she was certain none of her ideas were any good: "...I've thought, can I give up creating?"

Wow.

Liz is a published writer. She came in to the workshop with a beautiful skein of a novel-in-progress bursting at the seams with ideas. In fact, she arrived with three novels. I pushed her to focus on one. But at some point in the past, things had gone weird for Liz, and she stopped being able to make her work. That spiraled into major self-blame, even self-hate. That tailspin made it impossible for Liz to let herself even listen to her own thoughts and ideas.

Then Robin, another workshop participant who had recently published a *New York Times* bestselling comic, piped up: "I've been in a creative rut. Right now, I'm going fast, but I spent decades, literally, like you."

Stories of struggle with creative practice began to emerge, one after another.

Stacy, a tenured anthropology professor with many publications under her belt, now working on adapting her research to comics form, said, "I'm just recovering from a deep period where I was like 'oh my god, I'll never have another idea in my life.' I still feel like that a lot of the time."

Kett, currently under contract for a 260-page graphic memoir, admitted, "I had a big creative block for almost a decade after I dropped a project that was too big. I only got back into comics because I was like: 'Two pages. I can do two.'"

For all of these creative people, those spans of time not-working were the bottom of the well. They were miserable, depressed. This state of misery lasted for years and years. It only got better when they figured out how to get traction on their work, *despite* not living idealized lives of dedicated workspaces and guaranteed incomes.

So if you feel deeply uncomfortable, even guilty, over trying to carve out time and attention for your personal creative work, you're not alone.

Why you're here

If you picked this book up, you likely suspect there's a difference between you and "most people."

You're right.

Here's the difference: You have self-directed creative work you care deeply about, work you want to be doing, that *no one is telling you to do.* Nothing will happen on this work if you don't do it. Basically, no one will care if it exists, until it already exists. And possibly no one will care even then. At least, that's what you fear.

You don't even have to identify as a "writer" or "artist," working on your magnum opus in your atelier, to have this problem. **If you have projects and goals that will contribute to your long-term vision for your future, but that simply *won't happen* if you don't stake out the space and attention for them you're in the right place.**

Like Liz, Robin, Stacy, Kett, and every creative person in my workshop, you have to decide, over and over, to do the work, and then you have to see it through.

No wonder you procrastinate.

No wonder you struggle with lack of motivation and self-doubt.

No wonder all those productivity and creativity and writing self-help books you've read haven't made a dent in your resistance. There's no existing pattern you can fall into that makes this easy. There's no boss holding the reins, no teacher who will lower your grade. This is *you*, deciding and doing.

How does procrastination play out for creative people?

You have work you're yearning to make real. You have tried, but the reality is that you rarely hit your goals. Even *saying* you're creative feels guilt-inducing. Because doesn't that imply actually creating and getting shit out the door?

Part of you might want to just quit. That same part of you asks, "Why bother?" But when you try to stop, when you suppress this need to create, it pours back out. The creative urge doesn't cooperate; it's an open wound.

This dilemma doesn't mean you need to make your creative work the center of your life. You don't need to make a career out of it or get famous. Nevertheless, the human race is programmed to get great pleasure and satisfaction out of creating, inventing, thinking. Some people are able to scratch that creative itch within their more traditional work, and that's great for them (until they retire!). But for most of us, the job alone doesn't do it.

I also won't kid you: It's not easy to build your creative work into a real life full of complicated obligations to yourself and others. That's a life you don't necessarily want to abandon, and in fact you might like to improve it. And integrating creative work into your life in more regular ways has trade-offs.

But consider the consequences of *inaction*:

- Anxiety
- Busyness
- Guilt
- Distraction
- Feelings of failure

You picked up this book for a reason: If you could live with the aftermath of *not* pursuing your creative work, you would not be reading this sentence right now. If you want to be a reasonably content person living your life, you will need to resolve your internal dilemma by doing this thing. You're not going to be able to wish it away. Deal with it.

> **My mission with this book is for you
> to come to value your creative work,
> and to see it as the oxygen that it is to your life.**

I know: Doing the work can be hard, it can be exhausting, it can be scary.

Not doing the work? If you're reading this, you probably already have an idea what that feels like—and it isn't pretty. For Robin, it was misery. For Liz, it was life-threatening.

I am not saying writing your novel is more important than putting food on the table. I'm not trying to tell you it's more important than caring for your kids. There are higher priorities, and there always will be.

But for Liz, for Robin, and, yes, for you, finding a way to do the creative work is *way up there*.

If your first thought after reading that is to wonder how that pursuit will affect your other responsibilities, roles, and relationships in life, consider this: Your significant other or spouse will be relieved, even thrilled, that you're more at ease and more engaged when you're there, instead of stewing much of the time, frustrated and resentful. Your kids will be happier kids if you're a happier parent. Trusting yourself by believing that you deserve to pursue your creative dreams— that *will* make you a happier person, and happiness is catching.

Procrastination

If you had asked me when I was 25 what I wanted with regard to my art, my answer would have been to just make more of it. Frankly, it wouldn't have been all that hard to improve on that metric. I wasn't making much.

But if you'd told me that it would be possible to both make more work *and* be less tied in knots and anxious about that process as well as everything else, I would have jumped on that offer before you could blink.

What I really wanted was to be happier. For me, a major component of being happier was making more work. But it was far from the only component. Being happier also included freedom from daily anxiety about my long list of things I needed to be doing, freedom from guilt about not-working when I spent time with my friends, and the knowledge that I was heading in the right direction overall with my art.

I can't help you with the intensity and uncertainty that being 25 entails. But whether you're that young or a whole lot older, you absolutely *can* take control over your thoughts and actions and lead a happier and more productive life.

At 25, I would have defined my problem as "procrastination."

Procrastination is what we call avoiding activities deemed necessary either by us or someone else. **The key feature of procrastination is that when we're in the midst of it, it feels out of our control, like it's happening without our permission.**

Case in point: The other day, I was procrastinating from writing this book by—drum roll—watching this wonderful video* about procrastination by Johnny Kelly for the Royal College of Art. It portrays a litany of things that the artist does to procrastinate, including making many cups of tea. Then I went and made myself a cup of tea.

However, what you *do* while procrastinating is not what you need to pay attention to. That, in itself, is a form of procrastination, a distraction from the underlying causes of the behavior. Procrastination results from free-floating anxiety that prevents you from focusing, from the split awareness that you should be (and want to be) working on one thing while you're actually doing something else. Procrastination makes enjoying or fully engaging in either endeavor impossible.

Here's the thing: Procrastination is a symptom, it's not the disease. And this symptom presents as a result of a whole host of specific maladies.

What I aim to do in this book is to turn your relationship with procrastination around, so that you can diagnose *why* you're procrastinating in any given situation and proactively solve the root problem.

The key insight you will internalize is that *your actions are your own*. You can take control over your behavior, so that when you decide that something truly is important to you, you will actually do that thing.

You've told yourself you want to make something: a painting, a film, a comic, a novel, a proposal, a blog, a new business.

Why aren't you working on it?

Procrastination comes in many variations. Chapter by chapter, we'll address each of them:

- Self-blame instead of self-compassion
- Comparing your way to that of others and finding fault, rather than dealing with your existing reality
- Feeling overwhelmed and "busy" instead of setting priorities and deciding to face your dilemmas
- Perfectionism instead of taking one step at a time
- Distraction instead of routine
- Trying to force yourself to do something because you said you would instead of gaining clarity on what you want for your life now

* *https://vimeo.com/9553205*

- Feeling you don't deserve to do work that makes you happy

You may not suffer from all of the above issues, but if you're procrastinating, you're harboring a few.

The secret to getting past your resistance is not about getting tough and forcing yourself through. **The secret lies in defining root causes, taking them apart, and building support systems to buttress you against the specific issues you face.**

This is what not-procrastinating looks like:

- Believing at your core that it's your right and responsibility to yourself to make your creative work.
- Knowing that you have control over your choices and behavior.
- Having an honest understanding of what you actually need to do in your life, and knowing that you'll need to make accommodations in order to make time for creative work.
- Truly knowing what your highest priorities are.
- Feeling confident in saying *no* to projects and requests that don't fit your priorities.
- Making it easy for yourself to get started because you've set your life up around doing the work you love.
- Knowing the next step when creating your work.
- Forgiving yourself quickly and honestly when you get off track.

Yes, you can achieve all those things. Maybe not all at once and maybe not all the time. No one's perfect. Still, you can implement changes today that will make a difference, and when you start to make these changes, they build upon one another and self-reinforce.

Procrastinating does not mean you're broken. It means you're trying to force something through willpower alone that takes a plan and structure to achieve. The will on its own is weak. In Part Two, we'll build you a powered exoskeleton that will get the job done.

If I want one thing for you, it's what has improved my life dramatically as I've achieved more of it: a sense of peace and sure direction. In practice, that looks like less anxiety and freaking out, and letting go of, or at least diminishing, the internal self-hatred that comes with most attempts to make creative work.

The goal is not only more and better work. It's a better life, a life less anxious and more free. If all you want is to cram more stuff into your days, if you're not ready to stop doing some things so you can start doing other things you care about more, then put this book down and back away slowly.

I want you to be happier. You might make more creative work as a result. Being creative without too much anxiety is frequently a side effect of being happier. But I will consider my job well done if you just make what you're going to make anyway, but do so in a better state of mind, so that the rest of your life feels easier and happier, too.

What ignoring your creative self gets you

I was in Muji the other day with my six-year-old, and he pitched a fit to get a long, skinny pad of paper with check boxes on it. Not to draw on or play with. He wanted to make *checklists*. He's his mother's son. I always made checklists of things I wanted to do. I had them in sketchbooks, on shreds of paper tucked in novels, in the backs of school notebooks. I remember compiling a list of something like 200 underground bands I wanted to check out (and before internet music, this was not easy to achieve).

I would make the lists, but I'd rarely check much of anything off them.

People look at me today, with a pile of graphic novels under my belt, a podcast, a blog, a full-time teaching/department chair job, and say, "Yeah, that's all fine for you, Jessica. You're *different*. You're a natural at this organization, get-things-done, productivity stuff."

But it's not true. That productivity was learned. I spent most of my youth walking around with a ringing anxious tension occupying a major portion of my brain capacity, at all times.

It is true that I'm intense. That has always been the case, and it still is. But I didn't have a *focus* for my intensity for a very long time, and if anything that just made things worse.

I remember the first time I ever saw punk rockers. It must have been about 1984, and I was a freshman at New Trier High School in suburban Chicago. New Trier at the time had two campuses, one for freshmen and one for upperclassmen.

One day I was visiting the upper school for an event, and these two girls were lolling on a car hood outside in the sunshine. In my memory, they had blue mohawks, fishnets, plaid schoolgirl skirts, ripped T-shirts, safety pins, the works. Now, this was Winnetka, Illinois, one of the richest towns in America, so these girls were not exactly OG punkers. But at 14, I was fascinated. I was attracted to their punk look, and more than that, their punk attitude.

I changed schools the next year, and in my new school I attached myself to the punk crowd. Gradually, I became a kind of modestly-punk kid. I did spend my free time going to punk shows in Chicago, I wore a leather jacket, I saved up my money from my job as a hardware-store clerk (a very punk job) to buy comics and vinyl records... records I'd play on that turntable I was definitely going to buy very soon.

I drew all the time in a big black sketchbook.

At the same time, I didn't dye my hair much, I didn't pierce my nose with a safety pin, and I went to school every day. I got good grades. I didn't love much about school, but I felt deeply obliged not only to do the work, but to do it well.

Every time I was given a choice between doing the arty, punk thing or doing the square thing, I did the square thing. On the newspaper, I didn't do features, I did news. I took Latin, not Spanish.

I never took an art class in high school. It never even occurred to me to take art. Art felt easy to me, it was fun. Fun meant it wasn't serious, and I couldn't possibly be learning.

How would anyone ever take me seriously if I devoted myself to art?

I reserved my punkest, angriest rebellion for fighting myself. Against "giving in" to what drew me.

I had a boulder-size chip on my shoulder, something to prove.

I would actually practice walking around looking mean, so no one would talk to me. I'd walk into Mrs. Field's Cookies to buy an after-school snack, wearing a Walkman (often turned off) and the darkest sunglasses I could find. Just to be rude.

I was angry.

And when it came time to go to college? I picked a top-10 liberal arts school in small-town America.

It was a great school, but culturally it was just about the worst fit you could imagine. I arrived dressed in a rock tee with rolled-up sleeves, giant hoop earrings, and bright red lipstick. Seemingly everyone I saw as I made my way to my dorm room wore heather-gray college T-shirts and pleated khaki shorts.

From Day One at my college, I was in a rage against everything about its dumpy Midwestern ways. Within about three months, I'd begun the process of transferring.

During this time, I got a letter from my father.

My father typed his letters because his handwriting is so terrible. But it also did give the letters an air of distant command. He suggested that, because I was so unhappy and was thinking of transferring, perhaps I should look at art school?

WHAT?

First of all, whose dad *suggests* art school?

Second of all, in retrospect, it wasn't a bad idea. I mean, I have spent my entire adult life as a cartoonist, as it turns out.

But my gut reaction at the time was FURY. I was like, "I'm fucking smart, *Dad*. I'm not going to fucking *art school*." I felt it meant he thought I was unserious. Which, in all fairness, probably played into it.

My actual reply: "I'm going to the *University of Chicago*. Try and call me unserious NOW, *Dad*."

I transferred and signed up for Chinese and astrophysics my first year.

Astrophysics was a giant, anonymous lecture class—and by the way, it sounds cool, but it turns out to be basically physics.

Chinese was five days a week at 8 a.m. At the end of the second quarter, my Chinese teacher pulled me into his office—and this was not a warm, caring guy—but he was concerned that, as an East Asian Studies major, I really could not afford to fail this class. Which I was in the process of doing. I told him, no no no, I was an English major. He was so impressed by my boldness for simply attempting to take Chinese that he gave me a C.

It was as if I thought, by completely ignoring what made me happy and plunging into some of the hardest academic stuff I'd ever faced, I would finally, once and for all, prove something to myself and to the world.

And I did. I proved that I was completely capable of making myself miserable for no earthly reason.

None of this story is directly about "productivity." I was not productive. That's the truth. But more important, I was deeply unhappy. And I believe those two facts are intimately intertwined.

I felt disempowered and wanted to gain respect and power through achievement. I did not see how feeling empowered could possibly be connected to anything that felt easy and joyful, like making art.

I was not productive because I wouldn't let myself care about my creative work. I also wouldn't let myself care about my academic work, beyond performing to expectations, and it showed. I tried to tamp down and ignore my creative impulses, which put me into a kind of zombie-like state of half-living.

It was a vicious cycle. I couldn't afford to look directly at my loves because they were tied tightly to my fears. So I didn't really look at anything and instead procrastinated like a champ. Procrastinating amped up the guilt and fears and made it even harder to focus on the work. And around we go again.

As a junior in college, I had some dry cleaning to pick up that I let sit there for probably six months. I might never have gotten it, I don't remember.

The dry cleaner was *in my building*.

That is what living in a state of denial about what you truly care about will do to you.

You've got to live in a way you can live with

Eventually, I got my head screwed on straight. It took time, but gradually I became clear enough on my desire to make art and to write that I was able not only to devote my life to art, but also now to question what I was doing from a place of self-awareness and confidence: Why this art form and not that? Do I have to make comics to be true to myself? Or will it also work to write and tell stories in other forms?

You're reading the answer to that last question, by the way.

But to get here, I had to go through a major transformation: I had to embrace my desire to make creative work, to decide it was worth doing, and that I have something to say that's worth saying.

That shift sounds easy, but it isn't, and we often have to even fool ourselves into finding our way there. For example, my friend Donna has a blog. More precisely, until recently, she thought she had "just" a blog. At some point, though, she realized that she's accidentally writing a book via her blog posts.

Donna never thought of herself as an author. Still, every time she sits down to write short, single-subject, punchy blog posts, she finds herself getting mired in the threads of a big idea she's trying to elaborate over numerous posts, and it's killing her. It's so hard to get her brain around what she wants to say. Donna feels out of control of her own process and project, and that often means she'll write hundreds of words, but still end up without a new blog post. You can guess where that leads. She asks herself, "What the hell am I doing here? Why can't I just put the damn thing out? What's the point of having a blog if I can't finish a post?"

And yet Donna finds herself back at the computer the next day, hacking away at it.

Donna is in what I call the Dark Forest. We'll explore the Dark Forest in detail in Part 4 near the end of this book, but what you need to know now is that as awful as it feels when you're in it, it's an essential stage of creative work, not a sign of your own artistic shortcomings. I keep telling Donna: "That's what it's *like* to be a writer. You care about what you're saying, but you don't have your ideas fully externalized yet, and you feel incapable of mastering them." If Donna wants to go beyond what she's been able to do before, if she wants to express thoughts that were previously unthought, the Dark Forest is a painful, but necessary, phase of creative work.

Knowing that the pain comes from the work of being an artist eases it a bit. But it doesn't solve it, because this feeling lies at the root: *"Who am I to declare that this creation needs creating?* Who needs this thing, really? No one is asking me to make it."

That gets us back to the crux of the problem, and the reason why the vast majority of creative works lie unfinished but not forgotten.

The essential problem with making creative work is that you have to make it for yourself. *You have to want to.* You have to *decide* it's worth your time and energy. Once you are making the work, you can put it in front of people who might need it, but until then, it takes ovaries to declare: "Not only am I allowed to do this, but I must, and this work is what the world needs. I'm spending my time and my energy on this because I believe in it, and I believe in *me*, and in my ability to do it." Living with that firm self-declaration is uncomfortable, if not excruciating.

It requires enormous self-confidence to believe what you're making is worth making. Think about it: You do very few things in life that are entirely self-motivated and self-produced with little to no support from friends, family, or society at large—pure products of your own desire to act.

Society issues lots of loud commands: Get a job. Find a partner. Get married. Buy a house. Be a parent. Be thin. Overeat. Make money. Exercise. Binge-watch TV shows.

Society does not tell us: Spend time with yourself. Dive into your most individual, personal thoughts and feelings. Use those ideas to create new work, which may or may not help you make a living or even find a place in the public world, and do it for no other reason than that the act of creation is essential to your mental and physical well-being.

That is not a thing.

Looking at it this way, it's more understandable why finding room for creativity in your life feels so difficult.

The decision to carve out time and attention to make your work is a breathtaking act of ego. You're saying, "I don't care what everyone else thinks I should be doing with my time. I know this is what I need to do."

If you've been trying to create new work of any kind, even if you feel like you're failing at it, you have made that decision, somewhere, somehow. But then you also have to live with it every day, as it bumps up against other feelings—that other things are "more important"; that other people need you to do things that take up all your time; that you're too stupid or untalented to make the thing, and anyway, who gives a shit if you do or you don't, so why even bother?

So that's what we're up against. Let's be clear on the stakes: This is an existential battle. Existential, meaning: Winning the battle is pivotal to your existence.

Am I laying it on too thick? This is what people tell me about how it feels to *not* be making their work:

- "I ask myself, 'Will it even be worth it?' 'Is it all a waste of time?' 'Should I just get a 'real job' and get on with life?' These questions are almost paralyzing…"

- "I'm supposed to enjoy making art, or at least I used to enjoy it, but now I'm so riddled with anxiety and self-loathing whenever I sit down to do it, it's almost impossible to get anything done."

- "I sit in front of the notebook and feel like it's just too late for me. And that this book isn't working, nothing's working, everything feels like it's made of spiders."

Those people have tried to give up, to will themselves into not wanting to make creative work. That seems like the easy path. But all that path gets you is the impulse to wear ultra-black sunglasses and be rude to the staff at Mrs. Field's Cookies. Responses like the ones above are why I founded the Creative Focus Workshop, the online course I teach to help creative professionals and committed non-professionals alike take control of their work.

Maybe you still think that creating is a fluffy extra because, somewhere inside, you believe *what* you want to create is silly or inessential. If so, here's the secret: *What* you create is not that important in this context. It's not about the product.

I will never promise that exercising your creative drive will feel joyful all the time, fix your entire life, or make you money. The idea of always finding "joy" in work is kinda bullshit. Sure, there's occasional joy, but there's also a lot of pain and difficulty. Even so, doing the work will make things better, because it will make you more fully yourself.

The job at hand is to make it more about joy and to eliminate *unnecessary* pain.

When I quit resisting what I cared about and what made me happy, I suddenly discovered vast stores of energy. When I allowed myself to use my creativity, I made more work and better work. And most important: For the first time, I became fully engaged in what I was doing, and that's what began to make me a happier person.

That's the big goal: It's not "make a comic book" or "write a novel." It's to be happy. Have a good life. To have a good life, you have to realize that you have a right and a responsibility to this work.

As we'll learn more about in Chapter 11, creative practice is self-care.

Playing little league

Here's why arranging your life to allow for creative work still feels hard, even after you've decided it's worth it and you're worth it: No one ever taught you how.

You've finished school. No one is asking you for anything. But you also have no gigs, no clients, no fans. No one cares if you succeed as a painter, novelist, or designer except your mom, and she mostly wants you to be able to buy food and pay rent.

You have to find the motivation in yourself to build routines and systems that support your making work regularly. And if there's one thing our educational system does not prepare us for, it's self-motivation.

What do people ask when you graduate? Is it: "What's your big project?" Or is it: "Have you found a job yet?"

Before finishing school, how many times did you have the chance to practice the process of producing not just an idea but the whole plan for completing a project, and then actually finishing that project on your own?

How many times has that happened since then?

When you're in school, you of course learn the subject matter of your classes. But the meta-learning that you do over those years is about skills like navigating bureaucracy, finessing deadlines, understanding hierarchy, performing in exchange for rewards. These are very useful skills when you're working for a boss. But they are pretty close to useless when it comes to organizing your life around self-generated creative work.

My student Michael helped me crystallize these ideas when he said, "It's really hard moving from the whole first part of life, where you live within structures created by other people—I got good at navigating systems. But getting into self-determined work is really difficult. In your whole childhood training you're taught to look externally for guidance and structure."

This is why building a personal creative path feels hard, perhaps even insurmountable. You may have never had to grapple with planning and executing a self-generated project of this scale in your life.

Don't worry: That's what we're here for. By the end of this book you'll have a working plan and a system that will support you as you move forward. If it sometimes feels uncomfortable and way too hard, remember that, whatever age you are, you may just be learning this stuff for the first time. You're playing little league, but thinking you should be varsity already. Give yourself time to learn and get up to speed.

How this book works

Now that we all acknowledge the seriousness of the case, let's get down to brass tacks. You must take action, and the actions you take will have to be pretty different from those you've taken in the past. After all, if those methods had worked, I wouldn't have the honor of addressing you right now.

Here's how we're going to turn your desire to work into concrete actions:

In Part One, each chapter will break out one root cause for procrastination and give you a straightforward, simple activity that will help you address that problem. Note: I recommend doing all the activities in order, but if you prefer to skip around in a way that makes more sense for you, you won't break anything.

In Part Two, we'll still be looking at root causes, but we'll move on to designing a robust and totally personalized system that I call your "powered exoskeleton" to structure your time and focus. This system will be designed to support you where you're weak and prone to falling off the wagon.

In Part Three, we'll move on from root causes to how to implement this system in an ongoing and unobtrusive way, how to make sure you're making real progress toward your goals, and how to decide if these really *are* the right goals.

Finally, in Part Four, we'll talk about some of the other challenges you're going to face as a creative person: getting derailed, and the aforementioned Dark Forest that you have to make your way through each time you face a giant project.

This book is not theoretical.

It's a practical manual containing short, useful activities in virtually every chapter, including one at the end of this introduction, and you will need to actually do them to understand how this all applies to you.

All the activities can be completed in a dedicated notebook, or in the *Growing Gills* Workbook I've developed for you, which you can download from my website[*].

I recommend grabbing the Workbook right now and printing the whole thing out, so you'll be ready to rock as we get to each of the activities. Then, mark out an hour per chapter on your calendar. If that means that reading this book and doing the activities stretches out over many weeks, so be it. If you don't create space on your calendar for it, it's not yet a real commitment (more on that in Chapter 10, Your Ideal Week, Next Week). When I teach this in the Creative Focus Workshop, we take four weeks for the whole process, and that's with the guidance and structure of the live cohort. Don't worry if it takes a while to fit all this into your busy life.

> **A word of warning:**
> **Simply reading the description of an activity and telling yourself, "Sure, I get it, that makes sense. OK, next page..." and skipping implementation will not cause changes in your life!**

If you want to make actual changes, and I know you do, **you've got to face your dilemmas**—a concept I will address fully in Chapter 1—**by making decisions with conscious intent, and taking action.**

The dilemmas in this case involve trade-offs and sacrifices in the realms of time, emotional discomfort, and cognitive strain:

- The discomfort of facing things about yourself that you're not happy about or proud of and committing those observations to paper.
- The time it takes to sit down, ponder, and answer this question honestly:

---

[*] *http://jessicaabel.com/gg-reader*

What will you *not* do in order to do this creative work? ✸

- The annoyance of having to print out the workbook sheets, possibly involving buying paper or toner, and/or unclogging your half-busted printer.
- Making literal room for your creative process by cleaning. You might have to actually clear physical space in your house to do the work. That's a drag.
- The realization that you need to make a bunch of real, concrete changes in your life.
- The time and effort required to think through and then put those changes into place.

These are not trivial demands. Ask yourself: "Am I ready to take action?"

> **On page 3 of your workbook, you'll find an agreement with yourself to fill out and sign: that you are committed to making change, and you will make the necessary tradeoffs.**

If you feel overwhelmed already

I know I'm asking a lot. This undertaking may already sound ninja-level and, at any number of points in your journey, you may feel not at all like ninja material. So I want to say at the outset: The fact that this creative productivity stuff feels hard is not you being crazy. I've had plenty of students struggle getting through all these steps. The number of them isn't meant to scare you, though it might. Rest assured: All the steps are here because they can serve you.

That said, should you struggle so much that you falter and only succeed in doing a portion of what's here, it's OK: Even doing *some* of the activities will cause some change. So even if you fear you won't finish, and even if it turns out you're right, it's worth starting. Also, there's no rule or judgment about how long finishing takes you; even if you stop for a long while, you can always come back to it.

The last thing I'd ever want is for this book to become another thing you're failing at. If working on Parts One and Two sends you into a tailspin, my advice is: Skip to the end and do the Restart activity in Part Four first. Don't worry about your one big creative goal for now. Just get the churn and anxiety under control first.

If you find yourself procrastinating on finishing this book, that's totally understandable. The dilemmas I listed above are real, and they will bring real discomfort and even pain. Resistance is natural. But trust me when I say, from the other side of that looming gap, that it will be worth it.

The Heisenberg Effect

Have you ever heard of the "Heisenberg Effect"? Scientifically, there is no such thing. What we call the Heisenberg Effect is a pop-science mashup of Heisenberg's Uncertainty Principle and the Observer Effect from physics. Our common misunderstanding of those two ideas in physics runs like this:

> **The act of observation changes the behavior of whatever is being observed.**

As I said, not a real principle in physics. Nevertheless, the reason this idea has legs and probably sounds familiar is that it certainly seems to hold true in human relations and behavior.

Pay attention to something, and your attention will start to change it.

This is because you actually think or act differently as a result of what you see while observing. Changes take place because you *make* changes, not because physics mysteriously causes something to happen.

An example: Austin Kleon, the author of *Steal Like an Artist* and other books that encourage repurposing cultural fodder as original creativity, challenged himself to use his own *Steal Like an Artist Journal* every day for a month*. Austin was in a creative lull, having just moved into a new house and a new studio, and the idea was simply to have a reason to talk about his book on social media and maybe sell some copies. Fair enough. The problem was, at the start of the month, Austin felt totally detached from this book he'd poured his creativity into not so very long before: "The thing was dead to me, of course, in that way that things published are."

---

* *http://austinkleon.com/2016/02/29/my-own-journal*

Despite that, as the month wore on, even filling out various activities in a totally rote manner started to change Austin's understanding of his own work: "I lazily filled out the Krazy Kat exercise with some lines from *Waiting For Godot* ("What do we do now that we are happy?") and even THOSE took on autobiographical meaning in light of the new house."

Photo by Austin Kleon

I don't know that Austin's new understanding of his work will lead to other new works, but it could. At a minimum, it was creatively rewarding and inspirational as a warm-up project while he got moved into a new house and studio after a long pause in his work. "I found that if I actually gave myself over to this material that was previously dead to me," observed Austin, "I kept uncovering surprising things."

With that bracing example in mind, I'm going to ask you to apply the Heisenberg Effect in your own life, before we really dive into the deep-thinking part of this book. This will not be easy. As was the case for Austin, you'll initially find it a bit exhausting. You'll discover things that will not please you. But the mere act of observation will cause changes in your behavior. More than that, with these records in hand, you'll be prepared to make thoughtful decisions about your priorities—decisions based on what's in your actual life—when you get a little further into this book.

I'm going to ask you to track your time, just for a couple of weeks. (I'll explain how in a minute.) Here's how you're likely to feel and respond when you see the results:

- "Wait, what? I spent two hours on what??"
- "I'm watching YouTube videos. Should I stop watching YouTube videos? Or just write down that I'm watching YouTube videos?" (The answer is the latter, as long as you're having fun and not sweatily procrastinating on something.)
- "Why am I doing activity X three times for 15 minutes when I could probably just put those together and enjoy it more?" (Here, go ahead and Heisenberg that activity if you're inclined. Why not? Experiment away.)

All of these feelings are perfectly OK. Stick with it.

If I could postpone asking you to do this time-tracking until you feel more prepared, I would. But frankly, knowing what you currently make time for in your existing life, what your life actually contains, is an essential underpinning for making different choices.

Activity: Time-tracking

Find this activity and any relevant worksheets in the Growing Gills Workbook at http://jessicaabel.com/gg-reader.

Step 1. Print out a week view of the online calendar you actually use (e.g., iCal or Google Calendar), or use the blank template in the Workbook.

Step 2. As you go through your day, note how you spend your time. Carry the paper calendar around with you, and clip a pen to it so you don't have to dig around for one. Don't get super-detailed about it, just, every 15 or 30 minutes, sum up what you've been doing.

Step 3. That's it. Keep doing this tracking every day for the next two weeks.

To reiterate: This is not an activity you can just nod your head at and skim over. I guarantee that if you're not already time-tracking, you don't actually know how much time you spend on various activities, nor do you know how long you take to finish specific tasks.

If you're scared, that's not only OK, it's natural, and it's because this work matters to you.

You can do this. Be brave.

Part 1:
So, What's
Stopping You?

What we're doing in this section

You're here because you want to be making creative work, and something is stopping you. Maybe a whole array of things is stopping you. Getting to where you feel in control of your creative work is a matter of figuring out what, exactly, those things are, and what you can do about it.

In Part 1 of this book, we'll lay out the primary reasons that you feel out of control of your creative efforts. Core to understanding and defeating their power is the idea of dilemma. By its nature, a dilemma demands difficult choices. But the power of your conscious decision can break the lock that dilemma has on you.

What you'll achieve in Part 1

In this section you'll:

- Define and take control of your Idea Debt
- Contain your open loops
- Defang your Should Monster
- Claim your authentic passions

And you'll finish with a number of inventories and documents that will help you steal the power of your procrastination and overwhelm.

Chapter 1
Facing Your Dilemmas
How to uncover the specific obstacles that stand in the way of your achieving your creative goals

I had a student, Rebeka, who had a full-time academic job—as a mathematician—in a different city from where her family lives, so she spent only four days a week there. She'd always loved comics and dreamed of becoming a professional cartoonist, and she came to me planning to spend her free time in her work-city on a regular illustrated blog, submitting to a biannual comics anthology, creating standalone comics on a regular basis, and submitting to regular academic presentations...oh, and learning German. Because she's in Germany. She felt like she should be making progress on all of these goals, that she should be able to hit her deadlines on five things at once.

This is on top of her job, mind you. I pointed out that *she* was the mathematician and should start by simply adding up the hours available in her week. Rebeka clarified that she worked in quantum mechanics, which pretty much explained the problem.

In quantum-land, Schrödinger's cat is locked in a box with a radioactive atom that will either decay and emit radiation or won't, and the cat will either die as a result or it won't. The cat exists in a state of quantum superposition. The cat is *both* dead and alive until you open the box to observe the result.

Thus, in quantum-land, Rebeka's comics and blog and presentations can all be completed simultaneously, in parallel universes.

Unfortunately, we live in a world that functions according to classical mechanics, and Rebeka has no more than eight hours free, in a good week. At my urging, she cut her projects down to one. Plus German. She started to make progress.

Progress on a project changes everything. It changes the work—it exists!—but it also changes *you*. It gives you a power over your life and choices that so few people have.

This power is what comes of understanding your available resources and committing to making the sometimes painful trade-offs that will give you the focus you need.

What is a dilemma?

Rebeka faced her situation: She had imagined that she could do everything, all at the same time, but instead, she got virtually nothing finished, and lived with incredible angst about it. In order to achieve an important goal, she would have to decide to give up on the fantasy that all her projects could happen *at the same time*.

Rebeka took control. She made a conscious decision: She would focus on her one most important project until she finished. The trade-off in this case is what's known as "opportunity cost." You barter any attempts to devote time to all the other things you could be doing for something *precious*: deep focus and progress on the ONE thing you're doing right now.

This is called a "dilemma." A dilemma, narratively speaking, is not just a decision to make; it's a situation where there are several options, all of which carry serious, non-negligible, *competing* trade-offs. Meaning, when you choose one option, you specifically lose out on the other options.

Narratively, dilemmas are very useful. Characters facing dilemmas grab our hearts and attention, and we feel along with them as the struggle with how to move forward.

Dilemmas in real life are a lot less fun. The reason we love to see characters grappling with dilemmas is because our own real dilemmas are so freaking hard. We want to know how others deal with them, to help guide and gauge our own decisions. Do you think it was easy for Rebeka to table three of her beloved projects? There was nothing easy about it.

Of course, once one project is done, she can take on the next one. But until then, she pays the (opportunity) cost.

Every choice you make, every time you prioritize one thing over another, there are corresponding sacrifices you make. Opportunity cost, certainly. But sometimes the trade-offs are financial, emotional, or relational. Whether you are willing to address those trade-offs explicitly or not is beside the point. They exist.

Continuing to work versus staying home with small children is a dilemma many people face. Either choice involves both great benefits and painful realities.

Choosing your job over being home with the kids? You might experience guilt, worry, difficulty managing child care providers, the high cost of child care, lack of flexibility, and missing your kids.

Choosing being at home with the kids over your job? You'll miss out on money, quiet, prestige, and feeling effective and appreciated as an adult with an advanced skill set.

Even if you attempt to solve your dilemma by picking a third way—working part time—that choice also comes with trade-offs, requiring you to find child care for when you're not available while also suffering from limitations on your job prospects and reduced income.

Facing the decision whether to work on your novel or watch Netflix sounds like a no-brainer, yet if you drill down and realize it's truly a dilemma, that minimizes the guilt and anxiety of choosing. There are real benefits and real costs to each choice.

Choosing writing over Netflix? You make progress that will give you a sense of pride. But you have to live with the discomfort of facing your work and all the feelings that come with that. Plus you're giving up your "free time." Major willpower depletion.

Choosing Netflix over writing? It's a nice break and it allows you to share in the social bonding that comes with watching the new shows, but now you have to live with guilt and self-blame for the writing you haven't done.

The problem is not enduring the discomfort of the trade-offs that come with a decision. You're tough. You can handle it.

The real problem comes when you *don't* decide, when you don't at all understand and face what sacrifices your actions (or non-actions) will entail, and instead let whatever happens, happen. In other words, your worst problems result from when you have a dilemma before you, and you *don't* face that fact and make the hard decision. Instead you just close your eyes and do whatever occurs to you...which will almost certainly be neither of the competing choices at the heart of your dilemma.

The reason a fun activity like watching Netflix can lead to feeling horrible about yourself is not because you don't deserve free time. It's because you feel out of control of your choices, and that's because you didn't *consciously* choose anything. (And yet you did choose, by watching instead of doing something else.)

Reveal the dilemma and make a conscious decision

[handwritten marginalia: consciously choose to do or not]

When I was 28, I moved to Mexico City with my now-husband, the cartoonist Matt Madden. We moved as curious young artists, not for jobs, but for the experience of living abroad. It was an amazing time. I loved learning Spanish (most of the time), exploring the city, meeting our amazing friends. I also loved that the small amount of freelance work I'd managed to find on the side while working full time in Chicago could pay for my life in Mexico. The exchange rate meant even small dollar incomes would stretch a very long way. I got to quit my job for the first time since I'd started working at 15.

That fact had many consequences, both good and bad. One of them was a bit of both: Suddenly, my habit of sleeping teenage-late on weekends could happen all week long. And it did. I would frequently sleep until 11 a.m. or noon, noodle around until late afternoon, do a bit of work, eventually eat dinner around 9 or 10 p.m., either go back to work or go out with friends, and get to bed at 2, 3, or 4 a.m.

I had forgotten this fact for a long time, but recently I was looking at Matt's book *99 Ways to Tell a Story: Exercises in Style*, which takes place in our Mexico apartment and revolves around the question, "What time is it?"

In the comic, it's 1:15. But I looked harder, and I finally realized, it's 1:15 *a.m.* Matt and I are both at work at our desks, as though it's midday, but it's *the middle of the night*. For the last ten years or so, I've gotten up around 7 a.m. every day, so this was kind of a shock.

Then I thought back:

We loved to cook and eat and drink and go out with friends. That meant, in our schedule, that we often essentially knocked off work at the equivalent of "noon." No wonder I got so little done and felt so terrible about it. On other nights, I had to skip the fun in order to work, and I was pissed off to be missing out.

If I wanted to have nice dinners and a social life, and *also* to get my creative work done, I had to actually get my ass out of bed at a decent hour and get to work before lunch. *Maybe a lot before lunch.*

Getting there took *years*, by the way. I moved the needle bit by bit (and then had a baby—bingo).

The reason you're not making your creative work isn't because you have no time—and I'm not saying you're not busy—it's because you're like me. I was living in a fantasy world in which I imagined one day I'd wake up and have a room of my own, or a month off from work, or an amazing new laptop, and those external things would miraculously give me a personality transplant, and then I would just painlessly make the work.

Anne Lamott posted an article on Facebook that she'd written for *Sunset Magazine,* in which she gently, insistently, asked the following of her students who say they want to write:

> *What manic or compulsive hours will they give up in trade for the equivalent time to write, or meander? Time is not free—that's why it's so precious and worth fighting for.*

> *...If they have to get up early for work and can't stay up late, I ask them if they are willing NOT to do one thing every day, that otherwise they were going to try and cram into their schedule.*

> *They may explain that they have to go to the gym four days a week or they get crazy, to which I reply that that's fine—no one else really cares if anyone else finally starts to write or volunteers with marine mammals. But how can they not care and let life slip away? Can't they give up the gym once a week and buy two hours' worth of fresh, delectable moments? (Here they glance at my butt.)*

What are you willing to give up?

The first step in making the right call is defining your dilemma. One technique for this process is a system called "The Five Whys" that comes from, of all places, a Toyota factory. Charles Duhigg wrote about this system and how to apply it in *The New York Times*. He wanted to resolve a resistant problem in his life: He and his wife intended to eat dinner with their kids every day, but consistently weren't doing it. He asked "why?" five times, in order to get to the heart of the problem:

For us, "the Five Whys" worked in a fairly straightforward manner. We began by identifying a problem: We never managed to have family dinner. Then we explored, at the most surface level, why that was true: Because my wife and I always got home later than we expected.

Then came another question: Why were we getting home so late? The answer was that, although we intended to leave the office by 5, we often found it impossible to walk away from our desks because there were so many miscellaneous tasks we had ignored during the day.

That prompted the third question: Why had we ignored all those tasks? Well, inevitably, we arrived at work each morning just as our first meetings were starting, and so rather than deal with unread memos and emails, we put them aside until later in the day – and then, when we finally got to them, there were new memos and emails that demanded our attention.

The fourth question: Why were we arriving at work right before our first meetings, rather than earlier in the day? Because although we always intended to leave the house at 8 and get the kids to school, we usually ran late, and didn't get out the door until 8:20 or so.

And, finally, why were we leaving the house later than we planned? Because it took so long to get the kids dressed in the morning that we always left later than we expected.

So Duhigg decided to spend time and attention on the kids' routine in the morning in order to solve the dinner issue. This is not pain-free. Now he's got to get up a bit earlier, make sure the kids have picked out their clothes the night before, and ride them all morning to get them out the door. From my own experience, I can tell you that's exhausting and sometimes annoying. But that's a trade Duhigg is willing to make, and the result is the time to sit down to family dinner together.

The Five Whys is a powerful way to reveal the dilemmas holding you back from meeting your creative goals. If you plan something, and it doesn't happen— especially if it's a pattern—it's because there's a hidden trade-off in there that you have not identified and agreed to make. *What am I choosing to give up?*

The objective here is to focus on a single goal that you've been trying to hit, unsuccessfully, for a while. Think of Charles Duhigg's example: having family dinner together. It seems simple, yet it (repeatedly) wasn't happening for Duhigg.

Here's another possible example: You plan to write for an hour in the morning, but it rarely (never) happens. Ask yourself:

> Why don't I start writing at 8 a.m. as I plan?
>
> Because I am responding to email.
>
> *Why am I responding to email?*
>
> Because I check email as soon as I wake up and then I feel compelled to answer every Pressing thing.
>
> *Why do I check email as soon as I wake up?*
>
> Because my phone is next to my bed.
>
> *Why is my phone next to my bed?*
>
> Because I use it as an alarm clock.
>
> *Why do I use it as an alarm clock?*
>
> Because it has an alarm clock and I don't own another alarm clock.

Notice this last why is a bit different: it points to a solution that is concrete and under our control.

Five whys are usually enough, but it's not a magic number. You may need a Why more or less, but the key is to **keep asking *why* until you can ask something along the lines of "Why did this process fail?"**

The core principle of the Five Whys is to *focus on processes, not people.* "Because I'm really busy" is a mid-point Why, not an end-point Why. *Why* are you busy? What is your busy made of?

In answer to the final Why in the example above, we've identified a process that's failing. Using the alarm-clock function on the phone is causing a domino effect that leads to not getting writing done.

Buying an alarm clock and forgoing using your phone for this purpose will be inconvenient, it will cost a bit of money, and it will entail adjusting your habits. But when you're deciding whether you're ready to endure those inconveniences, ask yourself: What does it cost you *not* to write first thing in the morning? **You are already living with that cost.** what am I missing out on by not doing this thing?

Weigh the dilemma: Is it really more viable to continually *not* do your creative work than to buy an alarm clock?

It often feels harder than it is

Rebeka, whom we met above, still does all the things she had planned to do, but she does them *one at a time.* Instead of feeling guilty all the time about the high bar she set and failed to clear, she's realistic about her ability to fit her creative work into her professional schedule. The ironic result of consciously deciding *not* to work on some things until later is that she finishes vastly more creative work than she did when she started this process. Saying no to her projects—for now— and thus avoiding the "guilt tax" of misery and self-blame while focusing more fully on the project at hand actually means that everything, *every single project,* happens *faster* than it would otherwise.

It feels really hard in the moment to commit to one course of action and deny yourself the other, but almost as soon as you make that decision, it pays off with greater peace of mind, greater focus, and more creative work done.

choose consciously

Activity:
The Five Whys

**Find this activity and any relevant worksheets
in the Growing Gills Workbook at http://jessicaabel.com/gg-reader.**

The purpose of this activity is to break down the resilient, puzzling blockages that keep stopping you from doing the things you really want to do.

Step 1. Name one activity that you say is extremely important to you, but that you consistently don't do.

Step 2. Ask "why" five times, each time digging deeper into what's guiding your choices. (It might not be exactly five times. You might need four; you might need seven. But the lucky number turns out to be five a surprising percentage of the time.)

- Why? Start with the most obvious, literal answer to this question.
- Why? Name what triggers that obvious answer.
- Why? What's the habit that supports that trigger.
- Why? Get literal about it.
- Why did this process fail?

Step 3. Name the trade-offs involved in changing the circumstances around your goal.

Step 4. Name the trade-offs involved in continuing to consistently not meet your goal.

Step 5. You have defined your dilemma. What are you going to do about it?

cardio (walk + run)
I'm already doing yoga.
I hate my gym. / prev experience
Too cold to go to other gym.
(really boring
not enough to get heart pumping / not exciting

→ run...
- can't do yoga every am
- need to take allergy pill
- which ruins program etc
- out of shape

if don't...
- won't build cardio levels
- don't get mental health benefits
Run @ lunch @ gym in apt

Chapter 2

Drowning in Idea Debt

How and why we hold on to too many creative ideas, and how that can stop you from finishing any of them

You're a creative person. By definition, that means you've got a big imagination.

Whether you're someone who has a couple of huge ideas that obsess you for years, or whether you're constantly coming up with new, potentially awesome stuff, or even if you're someone who lets ideas come and go, not believing that any of them are good enough to merit notice, you know better than anyone that the only way you will actually cause those ideas to become real in the world is to focus like a laser and do the daily, weekly, and ongoing work to build them. And that's where you stop. There's a massive gap between knowing that's how the project comes into being...and actually doing that work.

Do you lie awake sometimes, thinking about what might go into your project—what the characters or environment might look like, or how it will touch the audience in a whole new way? Do you imagine what it will feel like to have this project under your belt, and what kind of effect it will have on your life?

Let me tell you about *Forest Lords*.

Forest Lords is a series of 10 fantasy novels, each a thousand-page brick, about the epic adventures of Greenleaf Barksley, elf proletarian, and his journeys to receive the Golden Leaf and save his homeland from the scourge of the Curse of the Titaness Denox.

The thing is, none of this series exists—not even *Forest Lords Volume One: The Elven Soul*. There are binders and binders of "lore." There are sketchbooks full of character designs (that look suspiciously similar to *Elfquest* characters). There is the vivid, lively picture the putative author has in his head of how it's going to feel to write a fantasy series that has everyone panting for the next book or movie or TV show.*

But there is no book. There is only Idea Debt.

What's Idea Debt?

Idea Debt describes a phase of the creative process where many people get stuck, sometimes permanently. It's what happens when you spend a ton of time picturing what a project is going to be like, and how awesome it's going to be to have this thing done and in the world, and how cool it (and therefore you) will look, and how in demand you'll be, and how much money you're going to make... and very little time actually making the thing.

I understand this concept all too intimately, but I didn't have a name for it until Kazu Kibuishi, the author of the comics series *Amulet*, introduced me to the term "Idea Debt" when I interviewed him for my podcast, *Out on the Wire*, Episode 7: "The Dark Forest":

> *Kazu Kibuishi: You have this dream, this idea, of this awesome thing for years. You think, "Oh, I'm going to do this epic adventure. And it's going to be so great." And the truth is, no matter what you do, it will never be as great as it is in your mind. So you're really setting yourself up for failure in some ways. And I try to avoid that as much as possible. Even though I have to be the architect of this sprawling epic adventure, I don't want to think of it that way. If I do, I'm probably going to ruin it.*
>
> *I used to go snowboarding in the winter. And I used to like hitting all the*

---

* As a matter of actual fact, there are no binders either. This concept was invented by Benjamin Frisch as a snotty teen to poke fun at the massive Idea Debts being racked up by others he encountered in the comics scene.

jumps. And when I would go down the mountain, I would notice a bunch of young snowboarders who were waiting at the top of the jumps. They may look like they're waiting their turn. But in fact, they're waiting there because they're actually kind of afraid to hit that jump. And what they don't realize is that over time, they're getting colder, they're physically getting colder. The Idea Debt of having to make that jump and land it and be impressive is getting greater. So that by the time they actually do it, they're probably not going to fulfill that dream.

And so one thing I learned is to just hit the jump or just pass it. Just do it in the moment. Or not at all. And so you can move on and wait for the next time.

I try not to look at the thing I'm going to do as being this amazing, great, grand thing. Because if I do that, I will probably not achieve what I'm trying to do. It would be like looking at the sun.

How do you know you're caught in an Idea Debt vortex?

If...

- You tell 15 friends about your screenplay idea, but devote zero time in your week to facing the blank screen.
- You buy a domain name, spend weeks or months researching and reading up on how to build a website, but you don't actually install WordPress.
- You have a drawer full of half-finished stories and novels and a to-do list item every week that reads, "work on writing."
- You've read 12 free online guides to blogging, built three editorial calendars, have notes on a dozen posts, but you haven't gone live with your blog.
- You have "binders of lore" and no book.

...you're living with serious Idea Debt.

I've seen many people struggle for years with Idea Debt. Carrying that debt crippled them. They were beholden to their 12-year-old selves, who had imagined their grown-up future selves as famous manga authors with a 40-volume series under their belts. But they did not have the tools yet to actually make the work happen. And so they invested more and more into this grand idea, making it less and less likely that they'd ever be able to make the necessary sacrifices to make it real.

They had *binders of lore*.

If you recognize yourself, you are definitely not alone. There's nothing crazy about having Idea Debt. It's the most natural thing to result from having big creative ideas, but no real plan for actually working toward making them happen.

only potentially relevant to me

Idea Debt Type P

There are two main types of Idea debt. What Kazu Kibuishi is mainly talking about is perfectionism. ①

After I posted my Idea Debt article on my blog, Kazu replied in a tweet, "If I knew I would write/draw 9 volumes before starting *Amulet*, not sure I would have started. Glad I did!" Of course he's right. Avoiding Idea Debt is about acting before you think too much and get overwhelmed by how hard and important your project feels. That's what Kazu meant. **Just take the jump.**

So many people let perfectionism stop them. You picture how great the project will be, and then you think about how inadequate your current skills are, and then you stop. Well, guess what? If you don't actually try to make the project, even with your current skill set, and learn to live with the difference between what you imagine and what you actually are capable of, you will never become capable of bigger, better things. It's humbling. But there is no bridge over the gap. The only way out is through.

Radio producer Ira Glass has this to say about the Gap:

All of us who do creative work, we get into it because we have good taste. But there is a gap. For the first couple years you're making stuff, what you're making isn't so good. But your taste, the thing that got you into the game, your taste is still killer. And your taste is good enough that you can tell that what you're making is kind of a disappointment to you. You know what I mean? You can tell that it's still sort of crappy.

A lot of people never get past that phase. A lot of people, at that point, they quit.

Most everybody I know who does interesting creative work, they went through a phase of years where they had really good taste, they could tell what they were making wasn't as good as they wanted to be. They knew that it fell short.

And if you are just starting out or you are entering this phase, you gotta know it's totally normal and the most important possible thing you can do is do a lot of work. Do a huge volume of work. Put yourself on a deadline so that every week or every month you know you're gonna finish one story.

It is only by going through a volume of work that you're actually going to catch up, and close that gap, and your work will be as good as your ambitions.

Look, it took me longer to figure out how to do this than anybody I've ever met. It takes a while. It's gonna take you a while. It's normal to take a while.

You've just gotta fight your way through that.

Get ready to hike up your shorts and be brave. (But don't worry, I'm not going to leave you to figure out how to get through it all on your own. That's what this book is here for.)

Meanwhile, look around: Are you really a perfectionist? You might have anxiety around finishing a creative work, but think about all the things you *do* get done—the thank-you email you actually wrote for a birthday present, the pretty decent job you did on pulling together a Halloween costume for your kid, your reasonably clean bathroom. If you *didn't* actually write your thank-you note, I'm not trying to give you a perfectionist guilt trip. These specific examples may not pertain to you. The point is, we all have areas in life where we are getting necessary things done. It's OK to be good-enough and just keep moving in *some* area(s) of your life.

So when you say "I'm a perfectionist, so of course I can't finish this project because I need everything to be *just so*," you're allowing your perfectionist *tendencies* to overcomplicate the project, raise your anxiety level, and cause you to procrastinate.

Procrastination is not about your character. *It's the manifestation of anxiety.*

I call that **Idea Debt Type P**. "P" stands for "perfectionism" and "procrastination," and how those inherently linked tendencies can blow any project all out of proportion to what it actually is.

Idea Debt Type N

Another kind of idea debt is represented by the second part of Kazu Kibuishi's snowboarding analogy: "Just take the jump, or *skip it*." This is what happens when you carry Idea Debt Type P for too long, and your life moves on but your idea hangs on like an albatross.

This is what economists call the **Sunk Costs Fallacy**. You have what feels like a great idea at some point in your life, and then you grab on to it with a death grip, making notes and dreaming about it for years, until it takes over your imaginative space. But you **never step back and think**: "Is this really, still, a project I want to be doing?" The fact that you "promised" yourself that you'd write your multivolume vampire epic when you were 15 does not mean you have to actually write that book if you're now more interested in, say, werewolves.

You've put in hours, days, even years of thinking and planning on a project, and to abandon it now feels like betrayal of your earlier self *as well as a waste of all that time and energy*. But here are the key questions:

1. If you do intend to finish this project, will you be able to? Or is it too far from your current interests to hold you? Will you be fighting yourself the whole time? Will you actually hate doing the work?

2. If you manage to get it done despite #1, what will the outcome be? Will it be something you really want and feel satisfied by?

For example, say you decide to create a short animation. You develop the character, you plot it out, you start creating key frames...and then life happens, and you're on to something else. But you keep reminding yourself that this is your big goal: Make this animation and you'll win awards, or attract the attention of a studio, or be able to pitch a show.

You force yourself to sit down to it again. But you don't really care about the character you created anymore. And you hate drawing the cells. It's so dull you want to shoot yourself. You make yourself do it anyway. You post it to YouTube, and someone offers you the chance to make more animation...of the character you are completely over. So, what, now you spend the next 10 years drawing animation, an activity you hate, of a character you don't like?

And that's the best-case scenario. Often, very little will happen. And you just spent three years making a five-minute video that no one is watching and that you don't love.

Why would you do this to yourself?

The fact that you "promised" yourself in the past to do this project is not important. Breaking a promise to someone who no longer exists—that is, you, ten years ago—is perfectly OK. It does not make you untrustworthy. You only have so much time in your life. You are not getting paid for this.

The fact that you've put in hours and hours on it already is also not important. ✗
It feels *really* important, I know. Believe me, I know that feeling. But that time is
gone, that ship has sailed. Do you want to throw good time after bad?

The more time and energy you've devoted to a project, the harder it is to
jettison it. That's the nature of the Sunk Costs Fallacy. It's a *fallacy* because having
invested in something does not make it better or more important than something
you haven't invested in. The key lies in finding the project you care about and are
excited to work on today, right now. ✗

Check yourself: That project you are telling yourself you were really, truly,
finally going to do after reading this book? *Do you want to actually do that project?*
And do you want to HAVE DONE that project?

Please answer yes, *enthusiastically*, to both questions, or proceed to the
next paragraph.

And if the answer is no? I give you permission to just dump that project. Or
rather, because it represents the goals and dreams of a certain phase of your life, to
respectfully put the idea to rest. Then start something new before you let yourself
think too hard. ✗

If you don't actually give that old project up (and the six others you've got
stored away, waiting), if you don't have a nice little ceremony and *truly* say goodbye
to these ideas, you end up stacking new ideas on old, and none of the old projects
ever go away.

We are **weighed down** by old ideas. If we don't truly shake free of them, some
part of our brains is devoted to processing them at all times.

That old saw about how we only use 10% of our brain? It's totally not true...
but if you're living in major Idea Debt, you may feel like you only have 10% of your
brain actually available to you when you want to make your work. That's not great.

Just as when you carry financial debt, which limits your choices about what to
do with your time and energy because you have to earn cash to service your debt,
carrying Idea Debt can cripple you creatively.

I'm calling this **Idea Debt Type N**. "N" stands for Nostalgia and how you're
letting your sentiment for an old idea and an old version of yourself overshadow
what your current self is truly interested in.

I've carried a huge amount of Idea Debt Type N. Many of the projects on my
"someday/maybe" list belonged to other, earlier versions of me, not to the me of today:

- Screenplay of one of my books? 2007. No one is asking for it, and I haven't been in that headspace since at least 2009.

- Ebook series of my unpublished YA novel? 2006. Does that mean I'd have to actually read it again?

- Sequel in a series? 2009. After the first one didn't work? Why would I do that to myself?

- Literary graphic novel idea? That one has been hanging around since 1998 or so.

You've grown up. You've changed. And when you finally kick all those old ideas out of the house—the ones you keep returning to and feeding because you feel like you ought to— you'll recover massive amounts of psychic energy. That energy is what you use to focus on the one idea you actually do want to be doing right now.

How to rid yourself of Idea Debt

OK, so we all agree: Idea Debt is bad. What do we do about it?

Our next step centers on taking all the extra stuff swimming around your brain, causing you anxiety, and *outing* it. We're going to make it visible.

Making it visible, on paper, is the first step to building a trusted storage system for all those ideas and tasks so your subconscious gradually learns that it can relax and not freak out because it's taking stock of and monitoring it all constantly. That's how you regain access to more like—well, let's be realistic—like 50% to 75% of your brain? That'd be pretty good, right? That would be a vast improvement.

The other thing we'll do with all that debt, in Chapter 8, is **we're going to make decisions.** They will not be easy choices to make, and you may not be fully confident that they're the right ones. It does not matter. You will make the decisions anyway. And it will make everything better.

Activity:
Idea Debt Inventory

Find this activity and any relevant worksheets

in the Growing Gills Workbook at http://jessicaabel.com/gg-reader.

This is how we turn nasty Idea Debt into beautiful Idea Investment.

Materials: Your Idea Debt Inventory worksheet or a small notebook.

This work is best done on real paper that you carry with you, keeping a pen clipped to it. You can use a digital tool if it makes you happier, but carrying grubby pieces of folded paper around, in your pockets, notebook, purse or bag, is a powerful, tactile way to make sure you have it always available. It also gives your brain space and time to percolate on these ideas. When I have a digital list, I'm tempted to get in there and reorder it, trim it, make it pretty... and you can't make this worksheet pretty. They are not and should not be pretty. We will get everything all tidied away by the end of the book, I promise. But see how far paper can get you.

Step 1: On the Idea Debt Inventory worksheet (or in a notebook you carry with you everywhere), <u>make a list of all your creative projects</u>: all the things you have swimming around your brain, nagging at you to pay attention.

That's it. Ignore the second column of the worksheet ("Potential") for now and ponder your list until you get to Step 2, in the "One Goal to Rule Them All" activity in Chapter 7, where you'll choose what to focus on.

- 5-min set your open mic
- improv class
- write comedy sketch
- acting class
- write web series sitcom
- write dramedy short pilot

Chapter 3
Open Loops
Identifying and gaining control over the many commitments you've made to yourself and others

Audit your desk, defang your space

Getting all your Idea Debt on paper and thinking about it feels scary, but it's also liberating. At least you know what all your projects are!

But the unfortunate reality is, those are *not* all your projects. As soon as you start thinking about getting down to work again, your brain will start spinning off into a million new directions:

- I've got to call Peter's school about parent-teacher conferences.
- There are dishes in the sink.
- *Forest Lords* is coming off Netflix tomorrow, and I have 3 episodes left.
- Joanne is coming over for dinner, and I have no idea what I'll cook!
- I have to pay those bills.
- I told Nate I'd look at his résumé.

- The laundry is sitting in the dryer, getting more wrinkly by the minute...

In his book *Getting Things Done*[*], those thoughts are what David Allen calls "open loops." Open loops are any tasks, projects, and commitments you've started (and "started" can even mean "had a random thought about doing"), and not finished.

Here's the deal: Our brains can hold only so much in active memory.

If you've got open loops, you're trying to hold everything you want or need to do in active memory, so you're constantly anxious that you'll forget something. Which is smart, because you will.

It's also dumb because you're practically guaranteeing that you'll end up living with Idea Debt's nasty little sister: worrying about everything you've got to do while doing none of it. She's no one's idea of a good roommate.

Wherever you are, look around you. Your life is full of open loops.

Are there open tabs on your browser?

Open loops.

Do you have a bunch of stuff on your computer desktop?

Open loops.

How many apps are open on your phone?

Open loops.

On your desk, how many individual pieces of paper sit there representing something you need to do?

Do I need to say it?

Here's how open loops affect me. If I have a thing I've mentally committed to, I end up constantly running over all the parts of it in my mind. But in the middle of running through the details, I'll have some thought about something else I need to do, and then I'll feel obliged to go through all the steps having to do with *that* thing. Then I'll realize I lost my place on the first thing, and I'll start over. Ad infinitum. At some point, I'll realize I've been lying in bed for two hours with my heart racing, sweating through my pajamas. Sound familiar?

Does anything pop out at you from that description? Like, why don't I just write it down? Yes, exactly. This is the key action I learned from David Allen, and it saved my life. I went from 24-hour-a-day anxiety and churning over All My Stuff

---

[*] *https://en.wikipedia.org/wiki/Getting_Things_Done*

to limiting that feeling to very short periods before I remember to slap myself in the face and say: "Download it already, bonehead!"

And then I write it down.

But what are you supposed to write down? What—specifically—are open loops?

Open loops ARE:

Open loops are those things you've started (even by just having the idea) and haven't finished that you have to hold in your brain if they're not on a list. They are physical things, thoughts, and ideas that represent a task or project to be completed. If you find yourself thinking about the thing or glancing at it and wincing, like "Oh man, I have to remember to do X…" or "Crap, I told her I'd get back about Z last week…", that's a classic open loop. Open loops comprise the stuff that occupies your active thoughts, the stuff you tend to ruminate on, run through a list of, or remember with a little start that you've forgotten.

That's what we want to capture. You will find them all over your workspace, house, and brain. Capture as many as you can. WRITE THEM DOWN.

Open loops do not have to be charged or emotional in and of themselves. The emotion often comes from the guilt or anxiety around not doing them.

Open loops are NOT:

Because they are unfinished tasks, projects, and commitments that you struggle to remember and that cause you anxiety, open loops are *not* regular tasks that you do automatically ("processes," see Chapter 6), nor are they about getting rid of physical things purely for the sake of minimalism.

In short, open loops are not:

- **Chores.** Things you have to do daily or weekly that you have no trouble remembering (even if you sometimes resent or avoid them)—"clean the kitchen after dinner" and "put the kid to bed," for example—are not open loops.
- **Favorite objects.** Things you like having around and looking at, and that demand no action of you, are not open loops. This exercise is not about becoming a neatnik. Objects that bother you—the ones that make you think, "Damn, I really ought to get rid of that crap, my desk is such a mess"—are open loops. If they don't bother you—"I love my giant marble Klingon head

sculpture, even if it takes up half my desk, and I will fight Marie Kondo to the death over it"—they're not open loops.

Open loops are SORTA:

Idea debt, that batch of creative ideas you've been kicking around mentally but don't get very far on in practice, is a different kind of open loop. You probably have tons of ideas *about* your ideas, like how to attack some aspect of it, what you want to do with it, etc. For example: If you're considering making a YouTube series, you might find yourself thinking about who you can ask to act, or research you need to do on video equipment, or possibilities for locations. We'll generate these ideas on purpose a few chapters down the road. These are open loops in that, if you don't capture them and write them down, your brain will feel obliged to hold them in active memory, and that's when you get insomnia from thinking about it all night.

They may not yet demand any action. Still, write them down.

Students in the Creative Focus Workshop ironically found this perhaps the most surprising activity they did. I say ironically because most people think their piles just need to be "cleaned up." That's what your mom has been telling you since you were a kid. But when you look at the piles as not just an assortment of things to tidy, but collections of commitments, you start to understand why they give you the heebie-jeebies and how they hide dilemmas. Students report feeling "lighter," "freer," and "less overwhelmed" just by naming everything they've got lined up. (They've also found unpaid bills...and uncashed checks!)

Building trust with yourself

The reason you keep all your tasks in your head is that you don't have a system—like an external hard drive—that you *trust* to keep it all outside your head. You probably have little notes to yourself and to-do lists all over the place. You may have literal sticky notes stuck to your computer. You tape a note to your lunch (and then forget your lunch) or keep multiple small notebooks all over your apartment, in your bag, at work... I've seen it all.

So although you are writing down those crucial actions, which is great, you may never see those notes again. Therefore, your brain, which knows this all too well, feels obliged to run through its paces.

In the activity below, you're going to capture as many of your open loops as you can, and get them on a list. This will become part of your trusted system, along with your creative projects, because one of the biggest pitfalls in trying to plan your creative work is not properly taking stock of what *else* you have promised yourself or others that you'll do. *what are all my commitments to myself + others?*

Promises feel urgent, so they end up taking precedence over dreams, which are *merely* important. You do the daily necessary bits of stuff, you tackle the urgent as best you can, but you never arrive at doing the things that are truly important.

"Urgent" and "important" are terms you may have heard together before, that come from a quote by Dwight D. Eisenhower, ""I have two kinds of problems: the urgent and the important. The urgent are not important, and the important are never urgent." This idea has been converted into a kind of prioritization matrix.

However, students in the Creative Focus Workshop rightly pointed out that this well-worn terminology ("urgent" vs. "important") doesn't really capture the difference between these kinds of tasks. Together, we agreed on new terms that feel more on point.

"Pressing" tasks really need doing, *or at least make you feel like they do.*

"Vital" tasks are connected to your core, your life, in some central way, including non-creative-work goals, like spending more time with your aging parents.

While listing all your nasty little to-dos will feel annoying and possibly beside the point, it is absolutely on point: We are here to integrate your creative work with your actual life; therefore, we need to take a hard look at your actual life.

Activity:
The Stuff Audit

**Find this activity and any relevant worksheets
in the Growing Gills Workbook at http://jessicaabel.com/gg-reader.**

The objective of this activity is to begin to catalogue, prioritize, and, when possible, minimize your commitments—both to yourself and to others.

For the purposes of this exercise, we're just going to concentrate on your workspace. But this process applies equally to all your stuff. I really encourage you to <u>continue the Stuff Audit</u> outlined below <u>surface by surface, room by room, until you have captured it all.</u>

But you don't need to do all that today!

Materials:

- Your workspace
- The hot, calming beverage of your choice
- An empty (physical) inbox (Make sure you start the activity with it empty.)
- A trash can and a recycling bin
- A file drawer or box and blank file folders
- (Several) printed-out worksheet(s) from the Workbook (If you haven't downloaded the Workbook yet, use a pad of paper.)
- Don't have all that stuff? Improvise. Better that than not doing this activity at all. I warn you, though, if you just make a pile of "to file...," that stuff will sit there way too long, possibly forever, and that's another open loop. If you don't have a filing system, maybe the "circular file" should be your go-to.

Plan to spend an hour on this. You may need more sessions (OK, real talk: You will need more sessions), but it can be draining to do this hard thinking about your commitments, so an hour is a great start.

Step 1: Get out your worksheet.

Step 2: Start to the immediate left of wherever you are right now, and pick up the first thing you see.

Step 3: Interrogate it. "Why are you here? What do you want with me?" Is there some action you, personally, can (and want to) do with this object?

Step 4: In order to help you answer those questions, in the worksheet, list the open loop, the thing you think you need to do. And then, using the categories below, you can check off a few boxes.

- Pressing (feels like a should or must)
- Vital (connects to some central value you hold)
- Both
- Neither
- I am the one to do this.
- Someone else really should be doing this (who?).
- Deadline _____
- No deadline

Step 5: If the answer to "Am I the one to do this?" is no, you've got three choices:

- Decline. (Say no.)
- Delegate. (This is someone else's job. Assign it.)
- Delete. (Forget it ever happened.)

Step 6: If the answer is yes, you will have two overall categories of things on your list that you want to actually do: things that are time-bound, and things that you want to do but that have no deadline:

- Date. (Put it on your calendar.)
- Do. (No deadline, but you want to do it.)

Step 7: Once you've done that, if there's some physical artifact that embodies the open loop, do one of the following:

- Put it in your inbox (e.g., if you have to deal with it, as in a bill you need to pay).
- File it (e.g., if it's truly something you want to save, like a receipt you need for tax purposes or a thank-you note from your mom).
- Put it in a place of honor on a shelf (e.g., if it's a thing you truly love and want to be able to see).
- When possible, throw it away.

Step 8: Proceed to the next item.

As you're doing this work, you'll notice that you're thinking of lots of other things you need or want to do. Capture them in your system as soon as they come up. Do not let them escape. That's your Idea Debt flitting around.

Once you've gone through your complete workspace, you may have pages and pages of stuff. That's OK. That's normal. We'll take control of this situation as you go through the activities in this book. But meanwhile, read through your list and think once more: Do I really need or want to do this thing?

No? Delete and/or throw it away.

Remember: You have only five choices when it comes to any piece of stuff that enters your brain as a possible task or project.

If it's not your job to act, you can do one of the following:

- Decline. (Say no.)
- Delegate. (This is someone else's job. Assign it.)
- Delete. (Throw it away and forget it ever happened.)

If it is your job, you can file it under one of the following categories:

- Date. (Put it on your calendar because it has a deadline.)
- Do. (The task has no deadline, but you want to do it. Further thinking required. See Chapters 9 – 10)

Buck up, little soldier.

If you find yourself resisting this activity, it's understandable. Be gentle with yourself. Capturing open loops seems like it should be straightforward, but it's an inherently emotional activity, because we have many feelings about what we've promised, intended, or hoped to do. In her book *The Life-Changing Magic of Tidying Up*, Marie Kondo minimizes and dismisses this attachment we have to our things and projects, the deep resistance we feel to even identifying what we want to do, much less getting rid of it. Kondo herself seems to have no problem throwing most of her possessions away, but she's an outlier.

Remember that I'm not asking you to minimize your possessions. That's someone else's book. (Kondo's, in fact.) I'm asking you to evaluate and minimize your *commitments* to yourself and to others. That, in some ways, is a lot harder. It also, ironically, involves your physical stuff.

Why "tidying up" is more complicated than it sounds

I've had real experiences with (physical) "tidying up" recently—cases that don't even approach the rigorous standard of Kondo's KonMari method, but that nonetheless made clear to me that Kondo's ideas are deeply problematic when applied to the messiness of everyday lives.

I get the appeal: Kondo promises that everything you own will fit inside whatever storage you happen to already have, that you'll achieve clear, open, minimal space. Who doesn't want that? (Well, some people don't, but it sounds nice to me.) But deciding what's important and what isn't, what to keep and what to toss, is not only about what "sparks joy."

In a kind of aside at the end of the book, Kondo offers an explanation for why it can be hard to part with things: They represent either an attachment to the past, or a fear of the future (or both). She sounds as if she doesn't see these as valid reasons not to throw it all away.

But that's what our lives are full of: things saved in case we'll need them, which represent a kind of fear of the future (at minimum, because you don't want to have to find or buy them again), and things saved because of nostalgia for what they represent about your past.

These things may not feel joyful. They may even be burdensome. But they are your memory in concrete form, and that's a tough one.

The problem with not making decisions about what you want to do with these things (aside from not achieving that fabulous clean, minimal look) is that many of these things also represent jobs, to-dos. And that's where this book overlaps with Kondo's. Jobs and to-dos are commitments to yourself. And if you've picked up this book, chances are that you have made a lot more commitments than it's humanly possible to fulfill:

- Books you mean to read.
- Clothes you intend to fit into again.

- Broken things you plan to repair.

- Unwanted things you intend to sell.

- Family mementos that you feel an obligation to preserve, but that you don't actually personally care about.

Those are all nascent projects, and your brain knows it.

To fully grapple with the closets and file cabinets and piles, to actually do all the things you have told yourself you intend to do, would require devoting yourself full time to stuff-maintenance and life-archiving. Having all those things around you can cause you to grind to a standstill. Everywhere you set your eyes, you see a "to do," which leads you to fragment your attention and energy.

Not-deciding leads to overload, and may cause you to shut down as if you've had an allergic reaction.

Donna Davies Brackett summed up this issue on her blog.[*]

Keeping your desk clear isn't about finding better ways to organize your stuff—it's about deciding what matters to you. It's about deciding that you are unwilling to waste your time and energy—your life, in effect—tending to things that don't matter to you. And most people think that's what they are doing when they put something in a pile...but it's not.

You have to deal with those piles sometime.

When you put something in a pile, you aren't declaring that something isn't important. You're saying "I haven't decided about this yet so I'll put it over here and deal with it later."

...Yet, at some point, you will have to deal with that stuff—and until then, you've got to put up with the physical mess as well as the distraction of being constantly reminded of these other things you need to deal with.

Life is too precious to waste on what doesn't matter.

As much as we might wish that putting something in a pile doesn't cost us anything, it does. Every time you remind yourself you need to deal with x, y, or z in the pile, or you need to find something in there, or you have a conversation

---

[*] *http://www.beautifulfunctional.com/desk-clutter-matters*

with yourself about whether today's a good day for sorting through that stuff—
you are spending time, energy, and attention on it.

Is it freaking you out even to *think* about your open loops?

Some tips that may help:

1. Remember that, at this stage, you don't actually have to *close* all the loops, you just have to identify what they are. *write them down, slowly* *physically*

2. Writing down all your open loops on a list—and knowing that you can set a specific time to think about them and close them—will free up some mental space (that you habitually use to juggle these open loops and keep them in active memory) to focus on other things.

3. By identifying your open loops, sometimes you discover that you CAN actually close a few of the loops very quickly—for instance, maybe some of these jobs can be delegated to others. Or simply dropped.

4. Open loops can be a source of procrastination material. That's where prioritization comes in. Don't worry: We'll get there.

The Busy Trap

Even after doing a full Stuff Audit, the skeptic in you may be thinking, "But that laundry is not going to fold itself!" Maybe not. And maybe no one else in your household is remotely likely to fold the laundry. This is a real dilemma. I'm not going to tell you folding laundry doesn't matter, that your creative work is more important, so let it wrinkle. Your creative work is, of course, more important. But being able to show up to work or school in clothes that don't look like you used them for a seat cushion may be a more Pressing issue right now, as the laundry basket sits in front of you.

You live in the real world. Showing up in dirty, wrinkled clothes is only an option when one is between the ages of 15 and 25, and either attending or working in an art school. (I know this from experience.) If that's you, mazel tov: Embrace the punk aesthetic and enjoy the free hour to make progress on your creative work.

For the rest of us, this laundry basket represents all the busy work that overloads your life and makes it feel impossible to carve out time for the deep work you crave.

My friend Tim Kreider wrote a *New York Times* article a few years ago called "The Busy Trap"* that I find bracing and annoying in equal measure. It's a good read; I recommend it. Tim proposes that our busyness is entirely self-imposed: "The present hysteria is not a necessary or inevitable condition of life; it's something we've chosen, if only by our acquiescence to it."

Spoken like a guy who does not have a job or children.

Tim is a wonderful person, funny and fully present. He also says, "I did make a conscious decision, a long time ago, to choose time over money, since I've always understood that the best investment of my limited time on earth was to spend it with people I love." This is true. For most of the years I've known Tim, he would spend the temperate months in a cabin somewhere in Maryland that had no weatherproofing (and in my imagination didn't even have electricity). He'd only retreat to NYC to stay with friends when it was freezing. He traveled, he made his work. This was, as Tim says, a choice. What he did wasn't magical. He just made a very radical choice that we could, too, if we chose to: Keep the nut very, very small. Live lightly.

I have a much more complicated life. I must and do take responsibility for that as a choice. I have chosen to have kids, a marriage, a house, a job. Sometimes a lot of jobs.

As Oliver Burkeman said in his article "Why Time Management is Ruining Our Lives"**, "Plenty of unpleasant chores are essential to survival. But others are not—we have just been conditioned to assume that they are. It isn't compulsory to earn more money, achieve more goals, realize our potential on every dimension, or fit more in. In a quiet moment in Seattle, Robert Levine, a social psychologist from California, quoted the environmentalist Edward Abbey: 'Growth for the sake of growth is the ideology of the cancer cell.'"

So once you identify which "unpleasant chores" are essential, you quickly arrive at things you choose to do, rather than being forced to.

You're looking at your laundry basket.

---

* *http://opinionator.blogs.nytimes.com/2012/06/30/the-busy-trap*
** *http://www.theguardian.com/technology/2016/dec/22/why-time-management-is-ruining-our-lives*

Here's what's happened to me: I have gone entire years in a complete and total state of frazzle, telling myself, "It's just crunch time, this will all even out." It doesn't even out. As time passes, I create (that is, I choose) new things that keep my life insane before the old ones are even wrapped up. If I have idle time, it scares me.

When I realized that's what I was doing, it made me angry. I don't want to live that way. My dream is to have relaxed evenings and weekends, hanging out with my family, seeing friends. I want to take summer vacations in which all I do is read trashy books and drink wine on terraces. Don't you? Doesn't everyone?

Why am I talking about not working in a book dedicated to helping you do more of your creative work?

I'll get back to this shortly, but what I want you to take away here is that the time you have in your life is the time you have. No one gets more minutes in the day than anyone else (although plenty of people have more necessary responsibilities than others, ahem, Tim Kreider). When you choose to do one thing with your time, you're choosing not to do another. So don't be "busy." Have priorities.

Here's what I want you to take away from the idea of the Busy Trap. Being "busy" sucks. It's dumb. It feels terrible. We need to fight it. While most of us don't have full control over our busyness, to the extent that it is a choice, own it. Try this: If someone wants you to do something and you can't, or don't want to, say, "That's not a priority," instead of "I don't have time." This will remind you that you make choices.

> **Here's a quickie activity that might just change your life: Don't say the word "busy" for the next month.**

Chapter 4
Self-Forgiveness as a Productivity Tool
Embracing self-compassion instead of self-blame

I've already talked about a number of different issues that feed the *behavior* of procrastination, like Idea Debt, open loops, fear of exposure, and failing to identify and face the dilemma of a choice.

But most people think of procrastination as an immutable character flaw. The problem is, when you toss all these problems into a basket and label it "procrastination," and then label yourself a "procrastinator," you imagine that this is simply your inherent state of being. It's who you are. That's where you get off track. Even if you feel like this is what's stopping you cold, putting it in that form is making an *identity statement*.

For example: You would never (or at least should never) say to a misbehaving kid, "You're a bad boy," but instead, "You are behaving badly. Cut it out."

In the same way, when you say "I'm a procrastinator," you're saying, "This behavior is a part of my *being* on a deep level."

Procrastination is not about your character. It's a behavior. You procrastinate to try to avoid confronting something that causes you anxiety because it's emotionally or cognitively difficult. It's a completely natural response.

The key to defeating procrastination is getting to the heart of what's making you anxious, taking it apart, defining it, and figuring out if it's something you can handle. It almost always is, if you're willing to face the dilemma and do something hard. (And if you're not willing, then don't keep thinking this is something you plan to do. *Decide* not to.)

Whenever I procrastinate, I experience rising anxiety. Pretty soon my inner critic arrives and starts bitching me out: "Jeezus. Just get on with it already. You're such a slacker. Don't you see how much time you've wasted already today?" What I have a very hard time doing, even though I know better, is realizing what's going on in the moment and forgiving myself for heading down the wrong track. I feel as though I have to punish myself by being really mean. If I don't punish myself (with *extreme prejudice*), then what's to stop me from doing this again next time?

It's like the deterrent theory of prison, which posits that criminals won't commit crimes if they know how bad the punishment will be (i.e., we're gonna lock 'em up for a long time, if not for life). And that works *so well* in real life, right? What's the recidivism rate, like 75 percent? What's your *procrastination* recidivism rate? Mine's right up there at 100 percent.

Punishment doesn't work.

If you don't punish yourself, you'll feel weird for a while, like you're getting away with something. You might even spend time punishing yourself by feeling guilty for *not* being hard on yourself. Here's the good news: The more you let go of punishing yourself, the more quickly you'll be able to move on and get back to what you really want to be doing.

The end of procrastination is not about trying to do everything. It's about *not* doing all the things. It's *deciding* between what to do and what not to. It's taking control over when you do what you decide to do. You can't make those decisions when your brain is screaming at you. All you can do is run and hide (i.e., procrastinate more).

Weirdly, interestingly, self-compassion—forgiving yourself when you screw up, as opposed to trying to punish yourself for being "bad"—is the most powerful productivity tool I've ever discovered. It's like we're all abused dogs, and we act out aggressively until shown kindness.

Self-blame versus self-compassion

Beating yourself up...that's never worked, has it? I mean, has anyone ever beat themselves into productivity? If you think you have, I bet if you take a closer look, you'll realize that it was actually just a deadline sneaking up on you that made it happen.

Giving yourself crap over not working is how you *dispel* your creative energy. It's literally counterproductive.

My student Charlotte spent most of her adult life hearing that nagging, internal voice of self-blame:

> [I heard] the 'OHGODOHGODOHGOD' mantra, like, all of the time... interspersed with procrastination and denial about where I was (because, in reality, I had no idea where I was in a project, how long things took to complete, how much time I actually had in a day...)

Charlotte always felt like a "slacker" or that she was "failing"—to the point where she had dangerous anxiety issues.

Week after week, with time tracking and externalizing those thoughts to build her self-awareness, Charlotte began to understand that nothing was actually wrong with her. She created and performed a new stand-up routine, she's choreographing a dance, she's planning her wedding. It's all getting done.

The process of shedding that self-haranguing "OHGODOHGODOHGOD" mantra is a slow one. It's not done in a day or a month. It takes practice. But it can happen. Just a few weeks ago, I got an email from Charlotte saying she finally managed to celebrate something small she'd decided to do...and then actually gotten done. She said, "I really celebrated and I didn't die, nor did people line up to tell me how selfish I was being and that I'm a terrible human being! Need to work on continuing to do that."

I'm giving you a lot of tools that will help, but the heart of it all is: Be kind to yourself. Just simply not beating yourself up over whatever you think you ought to have done, that *alone* is a productivity tool.

Be kind to yourself

Easier said than done. I know all this stuff—hell, I am sitting here writing the book about it!—and I *still* try to punish myself for procrastination. But if you realize you're doing it, here's something I learned recently that really helps: Don't quit talking to yourself entirely, just talk to yourself in the third person, using your name. Instead of, "You stupid slacker, what are you doing?" try, "Jessica, you're procrastinating. You've gone down this road before. Let's figure out what's going on."

In an article titled, "The Voice of Reason"[*] in *Psychology Today*, Pamela Weintraub described a study by Ethan Kross at the Emotion & Self-Control Laboratory he directs at the University of Michigan on how third-person self-talk could affect giving a speech on a tight schedule (a high-anxiety situation for most of us).

> *Those using their name performed better on the speech (judged by independent evaluators) and engaged in far less rumination after it; they also experienced less depression and felt less shame.*

> *..."When dealing with strong emotions, taking a step back and becoming a detached observer can help," Kross explains. "It's very easy for people to advise their friends, yet when it comes to themselves, they have trouble. But people engaging in this process, using their own first name, are distancing themselves from the self, right in the moment, and that helps them perform."*

The Should Monster

That third-person trick is pretty awesome, right? Yet the idea that you'll be able to shut your inner dominatrix up that fast is probably a bit of a fantasy. Let's take a more direct approach.

Somewhere along the way here, you're going to start to confront resistance. It may happen very early. It may have already happened when you realized you were on page three of your Idea Debt list.

You're going to start to think, "Oh, man, this is basically impossible. I'll never get through this list. What am I thinking? I have a family to feed."

---

[*] *https://www.psychologytoday.com/articles/201505/the-voice-reason*

You're going to think, "I shouldn't even bother. I suck at this."

You're face to face with the Should Monster.

When I first ran the Creative Focus Workshop that this book is derived from, the evil gremlin of self-doubt we all experience as creators got a name and a face.

Cartoonist Sarah Leavitt drew this little homunculus to hang above her desk and represent all the crap she gives herself—that we all give ourselves.

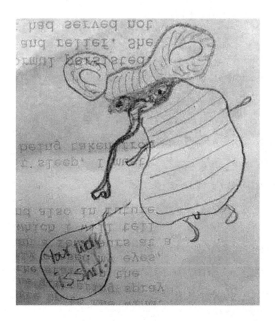

By Sarah Leavitt

And then writer Susan Olding wrote this fantastic list of her "shoulds." It's like a prose-poem of the shame we needlessly take on ourselves:

- *I should be writing every day.*
- *I should be writing a LOT every day.*
- *I should be writing less but better—perfect little nuggets of deathless prose.*
- *I should find a way to persuade my family to move to a really cheap apartment so I don't have to do as much paid work to keep us afloat. Even if that would totally suck for them.*
- *I should refuse all social engagements until I am finished with my big project.*
- *I should attend all writing-related social engagements even if I don't feel like going because that is part of being a good writerly citizen.*

- *I should volunteer my time to good causes, especially those that are arts-related.*
- *I should not volunteer my time to anything.*
- *I should be learning more software to improve my efficiency.*
- *I should be reviewing more books.*
- *I should focus on only one project at a time.*
- *I should not fritter my time on social media.*
- *I should get up really early to write.*
- *I should write really late at night.*
- *I should read more.*
- *I should learn Chinese. No, I should already have learned Chinese.*
- *I should go to the theater more often.*
- *I should listen to more podcasts.*
- *I should read and write a poem a day.*
- *I should read a book of essays per week.*
- *I should read War and Peace.*
- *I should write a series.*
- *I should write a bestseller.*
- *I should get my act together to send out more work.*
- *I should finish my novel or a work of narrative nonfiction so I can actually have a real career vs. what I have now.*
- *I should make my work more mainstream.*
- *I should make my work more experimental.*
- *I should be more like X, Y, or Z person who never seems to let anything stop her. Like, she has three kids, two of whom have serious mental health issues, and not much money, and a hugely demanding job—no, make that JOBS— and a mother who is totally demanding, and SHE STILL WRITES AMAZING WORK and she was just published in The New Yorker/Granta/Harper's, or got a three-book contract/awesome agent/invitation to speak or teach at this, that, or the other cushy colony, and just got nominated for/just won a GG/Pushcart/ Giller/Griffin. WHAT IS WRONG WITH ME??????*
- *I should just stop trying to make art at all because who do I think I am, anyway?*

Thus was born the Should Monster.

Now, just as we've outed your Idea Debt, we're going to out your Shoulds, and thereby defang them and take away their power over you.

Activity:
Outing your Should Monster

**Find this activity and any relevant worksheets
in the Growing Gills Workbook at http://jessicaabel.com/gg-reader.**

Think about when you're not pleased with how you're working (which might be a lot of the time). Your objective here is to identify the story you're telling yourself about how you *should* be working that consistently fails to line up with reality.

What internal expectations are you setting up that you fail to meet? You're saying to yourself day after day: I should be doing X. And you never do, and it makes you crazy.

Step 1. What are those things you tell yourself you should be doing? Make your list.

Step 2. When you've made your list, take a little time to think about it. Look for internal contradictions—for example, thinking you should do both a thing and its opposite.

Try to see which of these "shoulds" is connected to a real value you hold, and which ones are carried over from stuff other people say you ought to do, but you really have no interest in. Which are motivated by fear?

Step 3. Draw your personal Should Monster, and hang it above your workspace. (Or throw darts at it, or shred it, or burn it.)

I don't want to hear, "I should be able to draw better." Your drawing aptitude does not matter for this exercise. It also will help to make your Should Monster portrait as ridiculous and extreme as possible. This can help deflate its importance and hold over you.

Step 4. (Optional) If you feel comfortable doing so, please post your Should Monster on Instagram using the hashtags #shouldmonster and #growinggills. I think you'll find it rather cathartic.

NOTE: As much as many people have found this activity to be effective and helpful, some have felt too overwhelmed and besieged by "shoulds" to do the drawing, never mind hang it up where they can see it.

THIS IS OK. THIS IS COMPLETELY FINE.

This activity is meant to be really simple, just a chance to reflect on your inner critic. If you feel horrible even thinking about this, maybe you're not ready, and that's fine. Maybe you'll want to come back to it later.

Chapter 5

Authenticity is What You Actually Do Every Day

Acknowledging and gaining strength from what it is that you truly care about

I've been throwing around the word "trust" a lot, which surprises me. I've never been a woo-woo-mysteries-of-the-mind-and-universe person. I'm practical. I'm straightforward. But the more I work on helping people get right with their creative selves, the more I see that it really does come down to trust, to believing that you're worth investing in, that your ideas are valuable, that your mental and emotional health are high priorities, and maybe even that your actual work is needed in the world.

That's a tall order. It's going to take time, and, if you can get them, some external validation and help. (If you can't get that external validation and help, it's OK; it'll just take more time. You'll make it.)

One of the most overwhelming dilemmas you'll face when you start actually committing yourself to your creative practice, whatever it is, will be inside your own mind. This dilemma will stem from whether you can face your fears of putting yourself out there, of starting, of finishing, of being seen in public as caring about things you actually care about. You will have to decide that you're willing to be vulnerable in public. ✗

You're going to feel insecure. You're going to feel like you're faking it. You'll fear that someone will figure you out and expose you for the faker you are. (This fear has a name, by the way. It's the "impostor complex.")

I was listening to Marc Maron interview Kim Gordon of Sonic Youth (*WTF*, episode 588*), and this bit in the middle just knocked me back. Maron is asking Gordon about her early years. As you read her response, keep in mind that this is a woman who was regularly flying, by herself, at age 15, from LA to SF to catch rock shows at the Fillmore (in 1969, no less). This is a woman who then moved to the East Village in 1981, saw No Wave bands playing, and said, *I can do that.*

Kim Gordon: I go around thinking of myself as this really traditional, sort of middle class, grounded person. And I am a grounded person. But I... I don't... that's not my life, really. What I do is really more bohemian.

Marc Maron: You've always thought that?

KG: I realized that I still carry this idea of myself...that maybe, having a daughter, I wanted to almost overcompensate and have this really stable environment that was so square in the house.

I realized, why do I think of myself like that? Ha ha. I'm actually not like that at all, But I have that in me, because that's where I came from.

MM: Did that happen...that really must have just happened after you had the baby, right?

KG: I think I always, you know, when I moved to New York I was always like, god, I'm just so...

MM: Conventional??

KG: ...you know, middle class. It was just like fuckin' like, I'm never gonna be punk rock.

* *http://www.wtfpod.com/podcast/episodes/episode_588_-_kim_gordon*

MM: ...But you're so punk rock! I think for a whole generation of people, you're like, it! You're better than punk rock!

If Kim-Fucking-Gordon doesn't think she's punk enough, what the hell are the rest of us supposed to do? *"I'm just so, you know, middle class. It was just like fuckin' like, I'm never gonna be punk rock."* In the audio interview, you can hear the incredulity in Marc Maron's voice—it takes him several seconds to even absorb what Kim is trying to say.

This totally dragged me back to my own not-really-punk-enough youth, that youth when I went to punk shows on a weekly basis, collected records, and hung out with others doing the same, but did not dye my hair or get a crazy haircut, and was 15 to 20 years too late (and in the wrong country) to actually be "punk." But, I mean, what else is being punk than going to punk shows? Do you have to have personally known the Sex Pistols, and/or played in bands in the East Village in 1981 or earlier? (Like, by the way, Kim Gordon.)

What is authenticity if not actually doing the things you claim you care about day in and day out?

But like Groucho Marx said: "I don't want to belong to any club that would have me as a member." Part of valorizing some identity or role or group is feeling like it's hard to get into. If it were easy, everybody would be punk, right? And then being punk would suck.

My husband, Matt, told me recently that he has problems with the word "pretentious" because it puts down the very *idea* of ambition, of trying to be or do anything that you're not born to. And as middle-class American white kids from the suburbs (that's me and Matt, not necessarily you, of course), what are we born to? A kind of vague (though very real) entitlement and power, that nonetheless requires that we stick to our own kind, not ask too many questions, and keep our heads down? What if we have an ambition to be something else? What if we want to live in a more egalitarian way, or we want to do something risky with our lives that brings a less stable income, or we prefer to live in some other country? Are we then doomed to be posers?

Oh, the knots we tie ourselves into: I don't use the spelling of "poser" that I learned as a teen, "poseur," because although it means "pretentious" in French, to use French in everyday language is in itself pretentious. (By the way, I spent four years living in France. You do the math.)

I'm just gonna come right out with it: I am a poser.

I'm a cartoonist who didn't go to art school.

I teach using InDesign, but never learned graphic design.

I teach, but I have no teaching credentials.

I write articles that have no basis in research whatsoever.

I'm not punk enough.

My French sucks.

But you know what? I'm a good cartoonist. I am not half bad as a designer. I am an excellent teacher. People get a lot out of my blog even when (maybe especially when) I have no idea what I'm doing. I was front-person of a pretty decent band for a few years. I have French friends who understand me just fine.

Why? Because I did and do those things all the time, repeatedly, until they became a part of me.

You don't have to punish yourself in order to be the real thing. It doesn't have to hurt. My student Chad had a lightbulb moment in the Creative Focus Workshop:

The number one thing from this workshop that was different from all the other workshops I've taken is that it gave me at least some permission to call myself an artist. I think there's a lot of dangerous fetishization of work in the creative community. There's this worship of making yourself miserable in order to do a thing. And that followed me every time I did something new. Have I done enough research? Have I done enough practice?

I can't just do a project. As soon as I think about it, there's all this stuff that comes down on me: "I don't know enough anatomy. I have to study classical painters and how to do atmospheric perspective" and I think that the Creative Focus Workshop made us consider art as part of a landscape of your entire existence.

Be a poser. Be pretentious. Be ambitious. Try, even though it's way too scary and you'll never be in the big leagues and your inner authenticity police are sneering at you.

Be the thing you want to be.

Be a poser.

Activity:
What other people really think

Find this activity and any relevant worksheets

in the Growing Gills Workbook at http://jessicaabel.com/gg-reader.

Easier said than done. After reading the article on which this chapter is based, a friend of mine recalled an incident that has to be at least 15 years old, when she showed up to a basement punk show and some crusty punk looked her up and down and said about her skirt, "What is that, turquoise? Color! Crazy."

The authenticity police exist. They will come out and try to regulate you. And it will hurt enough that you remember 15 years later.

But what it comes down to is that guy was so concerned about his own punk-enoughness that he had to go around demonstrating that he knew the "rules" and was ready to defend them. Pushing people out of the circle is essential to insecure people who want to make sure the circle has edges and they are safely inside.

My friend, fortunately, shook it off and became a very successful adult who lives by her own creative rules. She's drawn her own circle.

If you find yourself worrying about what other people think, consider Brené Brown's 1-inch-square piece of paper. Brené Brown researches, writes, and speaks about the role of vulnerability in leadership (and, not incidentally, art). We creative people have given ourselves the job of revealing what we really think and feel *all the time* through our work. That is a very risky thing to do. It's natural that it would be scary to think about other people having *opinions* about it/us.

But when I feel this fear (and believe me, I do), I try to think through and identify who, exactly, I'm worried about. There are usually one or two people

I'm thinking of who might scoff at my project, whatever it is. And when I do identify those people? I usually realize I couldn't give a toss what they think. They don't matter to me.

This is where Brené Brown's 1-inch piece of paper comes in. Brown keeps an actual, literal 1-inch square of paper in her wallet, on which she's written the names of the people in her life whose opinions truly matter to her. They all fit. I bet if you try it, you'll find that's the case for you as well.

Step 1. Measure and cut out a 1-inch square of paper. Write the names of everyone whose opinions truly matter to you on the paper. Put it in your wallet.

Step 2. Consult your 1-inch-square paper whenever you start to think "people" will hate what you're doing or saying, and develop a more nuanced view of which "people" you're thinking of. There may be moments when your mom or, like, the Pope, would actually hate what you're doing, and, if they're on your paper, take time to consider that and decide if that matters enough to change what you're working on.

Otherwise? Brush it off.

Part 2: Build Your Custom-Powered Exoskeleton

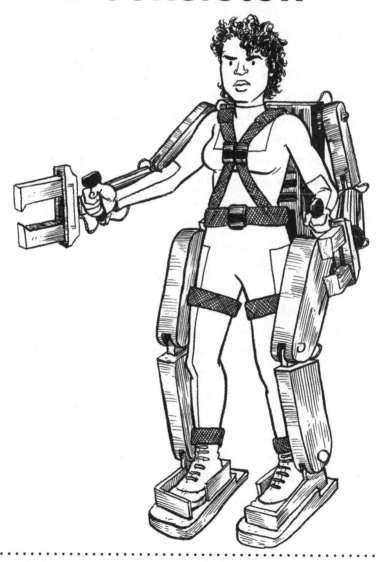

What we're doing in this section

In Part 1, I challenged you to take a hard look in the mirror. By documenting the parts of your creative life, but not doing anything to make change, you've essentially opened hella new loops, projects that you've begun and not finished. The good news is, now you've got the following inventories to work with, and they'll let you close those loops through conscious decisions:

- Time-tracking
- Dilemma analysis (5 whys)
- Idea Debt inventory
- Open loops list

According to our pseudo-scientific understanding of the Heisenberg Effect, you may have made some changes in your behavior without concretely planning to do so. Now it's time to get intentional about those changes...and close some loops.

In this section of the book, we're going to take all the thinking and record-keeping you've been doing, and we'll begin to build your custom- powered exoskeleton system that will help keep you on track and moving forward toward your real goals. You're going to build your resilience and resistance to the temptation to procrastinate, and you're going to make conscious choices about what in your real life you want to build up, and what you want to break down.

In short: You will take control of your priorities and your decision-making, and you'll align your activity more closely with how you really want to be spending your days.

What you'll achieve in Part 2:

- You'll learn why and how to choose one goal at a time, and what that means for all the other stuff you want to be doing. Then you'll actually make that choice.
- Next, you'll take your own big goal, which has seemed overwhelming and possibly *too* ambitious, and you'll break it down into daily, achievable actions.
- Then, you'll set up a system to schedule and track your progress on your project, using your time-tracking and, importantly, your growing understanding of how you've been most successful in the past.

When you finish this section of the book, you'll know exactly what to do with your time next week so that your project starts to take shape before your eyes.

Chapter 6
Prioritize
One Goal To Rule Them All
How to grapple with your many creative ideas and priorities

If you're like most creative people, you won't have just one idea simmering, waiting to be born. You'll have more like 12.

Here's what often happens: You're working on a project, a book, for example. You're excited about the idea, developing the outline, starting to rough out scenes. Things start to get more complicated. They slow down. It becomes harder to feel excited about the project moment to moment, and you start to doubt your judgment about it.

Meanwhile, you're hanging out with friends at a party, and you come up with this hilarious, awesome new idea. Not only is this new one way more fun to think about than the old one, you also start to feel like you need to do it, like you owe it to yourself. This idea could be the one that changes things for you. You start to make some notes.

But. You can't give up the first project. You're already stuck in, it's a solid idea, you know what potential it has...and so you start to juggle both projects.

Rinse and repeat.

Sound familiar?

My student Amy called the new projects that pop up and take over her "slutty new ideas."

New Idea doesn't have to go to work! New Idea doesn't have emotional baggage! All New Idea wants to do is lie around in bed, make pancakes, and make out.

The trouble is, that New Idea becomes Old Idea pretty fast, once you see her without her makeup, and she's used up all her date-underwear and now it's all Hanes Her Way and undereye bags.

A couple years ago, after I'd started writing about procrastination and helping creative people get more work done, I started to see a trend in the material I was reading for context and research.

One goal. *Have only one goal at a time.*

At first, this seemed kind of nutty. Maybe it would be a good idea for other people, but it didn't seem really necessary, for me at least. After all, I've always had multiple giant projects running in parallel, and I've gotten them done...eventually. But the idea kept coming up, and I started to let my defenses down a bit, and see the sense in it.

Why to say no

Imagine you figure out your schedule, and realize you have maybe eight hours a week for creative work outside your day job, if you're careful. You have eight projects. So you put in one hour on each. Seems logical, right? But really: How far or deep are you going to get?

OK, now imagine you spend eight hours over the course of a week on ONE project. You might get a whole chapter drafted in eight hours. Stranger things have happened. If you're spending chunks of time all week on the same project, your brain is going to be working overtime on it. When you're in the shower: brainstorm. When you're in the car, pieces are clicking together. Have your notebook or voice notes app handy. You will have ideas. I guarantee it.

working on one idea @ a time helps w/ incubation + inspiration @ all times

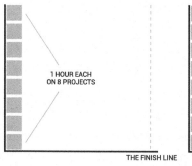

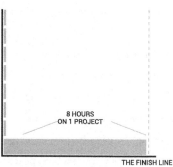

If you follow this pattern for anywhere between a month and a year or so, depending on the project: The thing is done. Actually done. You did it. Good lord. Imagine the party you'd throw to celebrate *that*.

What would it be like to have a big project completed and in the world? What would that do for your self-esteem? How might it connect you to other people? What kinds of professional opportunities might come up as a result?

How I realized I needed
to say no a lot more

In late 2015, I had a million things going on, and I felt harried and *busy* all the time. You know how I feel about "busy." It sucks. I was in the midst of producing the *Out on the Wire* podcast, on a schedule and with a collaborator, Benjamin Frisch, so that became my first priority. Everything else, including writing blog posts and planning my intercontinental move (from France to the USA in the summer of 2016), got the crumbs of my effort and attention. I flitted from one project to the next, nibbling away at the corners of each.

It was probably fine—the right choice—for an important creative project like the podcast to take precedence over blog posts and admin. But sitting right there beside all that was a giant kahuna of a project that took up (and still takes up!) a huge portion of my mental capacity: *Trish Trash: Rollergirl of Mars*.

Trish Trash is my sci-fi graphic novel about a 15-year-old girl who wants to be a derby star on Mars. (Because, of course, roller derby will be the number-one sport of the future. Natch.) The first volume of *Trish* came out in the U.S. in November 2016, which was great. The problem? I started this book in 2007. Actually, it was Christmas of 2006. By the time the first three volumes of the story come out, it will have been cooking for 12 years.

Holy crap!

At some point in 2012 or so, I went back and reconstructed my timeline of making this book, and I couldn't believe how long it had been. Then. Already. In 2012.

Why has it taken me so long? Well, the pages take a long time to draw, yes, and writing the script is demanding. But the real reason is illustrated by what was happening the day I had my forehead-smacking moment with my own situation. That day, I was writing a blog post about having one goal. (Ironic, right?) I was working on writing my Creative Focus Workshop course materials. I had calls to make to international shippers. I had scheduled writing two media pitch letters and penciling two pages of *Trish Trash* vol. 3. I also had about 20 other small items on my list. Here's what I wrote at the time:

> *What am I trying to do this week? Write this blog series, outline my book* [that's this book, by the way. Ten months before I actually *did* outline it.], *thumbnail 10 pages of my next comic, send out two media inquiries, look into shipping all our crap to the USA, _____. I mean, it's comical. I can't really do all that stuff. It's not possible.*

What *did* I finish? The blog post. I also made a bit of progress on the podcast script. Maybe five or six small to-dos on my list. That's it.

If I had chosen not to write a post, and not to do a podcast, I could have finished two or three pages of *Trish* pencils. But that wouldn't have been necessary, because if I'd started homing in on one goal back in late 2006, rather than trying to juggle umpteen of them all at once, *Trish would have already been finished years earlier.*

If I had been concentrating on only *Trish Trash* in 2007 and 2008, I'd have had it finished in 2009 at the outside.

What would that have meant for me? I'd have a 200-page sci-fi book published, I'd have been building readership, possibly leading to opportunities to make derivative works (such as animation or film), contemplating sequels...and I also wouldn't be drawing it *now*, when I've got other stuff I really want to be focusing on.

Too many projects = no projects

For years, I've been telling myself I can do it all. I'll fit it in. And I do, sort of, eventually. Ten months after writing that note to myself, I actually scheduled time on my calendar and outlined this book. (Which is to say, I finally faced the dilemma of what to focus on, and decided to make this book my priority—meaning *other* things took a back seat. Then I embodied that decision in my calendar.)

Thinking I wanted to do it the previous January did not make it happen any sooner. In fact, it might have actually delayed this project. Here's why: The moment it was a task on my to-do list, I began to feel a day-to-day gnawing guilt and drag on my awareness from *not* doing it, which accumulated into a major toll on my energy for doing what I actually was doing.

Having a red past-due item on my to-do list does no one any good. I feel like I never, ever get enough done, I feel busy and crappy, and meanwhile, you don't get a book to read.

If I'm realistic about my time, I will feel better about what I have achieved in a day, and that will lend me more energy to get back to it tomorrow. It will give me clarity about what I'm doing now, and what I want to do next. *be realistic about the time I have*

The reality is: You can't "fit it in," not if you don't have empty slots sitting on your calendar right now. All you can do is either add it to the back of the queue, or kick something else off your calendar for today. **That's not *fitting it in*, that's *choosing* to do something different.** And is that new shiny idea really what you want to choose? Or did it just bushwhack you?

Pick one goal at a time

Sure, pick one goal. Easy for me to say. I know: All your projects are on your list for a reason. Your projects are your creative babies. You've been carrying them in backpacks and slings and on your shoulders and on your hip...sometimes for years on end. They **all** matter to you. You're "multi-passionate." You have many goals. I get it.

I am not asking you to throw away your dreams. I'm asking you to concentrate on *one thing at a time*. Having lots of ambitious goals is great—just do them *sequentially* instead of *simultaneously*. *do goals sequentially*

OK, then, how do you make the decision? *understand how to write + perform comedy*

There's no one answer here, and it largely depends on what's driving your *what makes a/t/story* decisions and choices during that period in your life:

ℕ **Sometimes, you decide based on what will gain you small wins.** In my case, for example, if I sit here and get all the way through this chapter right now, then I will be on track to publish this book on schedule, and that will also make it possible to concentrate on *Trish Trash* later in the coming weeks.

↱ **Sometimes, you make the decision around money.** The truth is, even if I'd realized all this stuff back in 2007, I could not have concentrated on *Trish Trash* in 2007 and 2008 because I was already in the midst of writing *Drawing Words & Writing Pictures* and then *Mastering Comics*, my two textbooks on comics. And I was doing *that* because I got decent advances for those projects and had to pay my bills. *Trish Trash* would not pay my bills until I signed a contract, and that didn't happen until 2008. Decision made.

◈ **Sometimes, the decision is about developing a project that feeds your future self.** Often you know going in that it will take a huge time and energy investment, but you choose it because you're confident you'll be proud of it and yourself in the future. It will create new opportunities for you and build a new road into the future.

That's why in 2011 I took on *Out on the Wire* while still inching forward on *Trish Trash*. It added three more years to my timeline, but it was completely worth it to engage so deeply with great radio and podcast producers, to enrich my own creative work with new insights on narrative, and to create a statement about building narrative that can form the heart of a new conversation with readers and other professionals.

It was worth it to me, *but it came at a cost*. It turned what had been a current, exciting project for me into Idea Debt.

Trish Trash? I love this book, but I finished it emotionally, mentally, at least three years ago.

Is that a cost you'd be willing to pay?

And maybe knowing the answer to that question comes down to feeding your present creative self. When I started *Out on the Wire*, I was not only thinking about how it would build my future. I was also excited and intrigued by the actual creative problem at hand: how to uncover and then encapsulate something concrete, real, and helpful about how the best audio producers in the world consistently produce their amazing stories. (And on top of that, how to do so in comics form.) Not a simple problem, but one that lit me up and kept me going through my long journey through the Dark Forest.

There will always be things you could be doing that claim to be More Important or More Serious or More Needed in Our Current Political Age or whatever. Give yourself permission to feed yourself creatively; choose what actually inspires you and you'll be able to continue making the work even when the going gets tough.

Telling yourself that you'll just do a bit on this thing and a bit on that, that you'll fit it in, is a recipe for ending up with very little finished, at least not for a long, long time. And you're likely to lose steam completely on some projects. When you don't finish a project, you end up feeling like you're not working hard enough, so you hate yourself a little bit, or maybe a lot. You blame yourself, and you say, "I just need to work a little harder." But there is no point at which you find enough time to do all the projects, all at once, so the well of self-blame that goes with this reality has no bottom.

Choose one thing and go all in.

Choose one thing and it will set you free.

Choose One Thing. That's a great campaign slogan, but building it out into workable legislation is a more complicated issue. You will, no doubt, already be thinking about all the ways it won't work, or that it will be complicated for you. I'll cover most of those objections later in this chapter.

First, when I say "thing" what does that mean? You're literally supposed to do only one activity all day and night? Obviously, that's not going to work. So we'll start by defining terms.

Once you're clear on what you're trying to decide, you'll start to figure out what criteria are important to you and how to focus on the right aspects of a project.

Finally, deciding to do one thing means, necessarily, deciding not to do lots of other things. But saying no to others and to yourself is a whole skill unto itself. You'll master some tools to do this kindly and decisively.

Projects versus processes

In Part One, I took great pains to acknowledge that your life is complicated, and you may have very legit reasons that you want it to *remain* pretty complicated—parenting, having friends, keeping a demanding job, maintaining a hobby you're passionate about... "So what's all this about simplifying and choosing one thing to focus on? I thought this book was pro-multi-passionate!"

The key distinction to master is the difference between projects and processes.

A process is anything you do, and have done many times before, that doesn't now require enormous amounts of strategy and planning to make happen. It is a repeatable series of actions and procedures that you already understand. A process can be difficult, it can be unpleasant, but it's *known*.

Doing the functions of your job, getting your kids up and out the door for school—these things take energy and time, but they don't take creating new plans and learning new skills each and every time. Now, if something at work, for instance, is really off, like your weekly status meeting is annoying and ineffective, you might create a project around that. You could identify what result you need to see from the meeting, then use the five-whys technique to figure out why you're not getting that result, then rework the system. That's a project.

A project has a beginning, a middle, and an end, but perhaps more important, a project has unanswered questions at the heart of it.

By their nature, many creative projects are just that: projects. You're creating something new, and that entails unanswered questions. But your creative work does not have to consist of "projects" only. You may also have processes in place. If you're in the midst of a long series of similar works, you may have worked out a process for creating them that takes most of the guesswork out of the job. Then all you need to do is put the time for executing the process on the calendar, and you're good to go. Usually, the unknowns are what stop us. That's why the rule is: One *project* at a time. Focus on one new project under active development (while you continue to run the processes that are necessary for your life to function alongside).

How much is too much?

Of course, in order to clear time for your big ambitious projects, you may need to take a hard look at your *processes*, and make some decisions about which are really necessary, and how often. Does your rug need vacuuming every week, or can you wait two? Just as you have time and headspace for only so many projects, you also have a time-and-energy limit for processes. That will entail saying no to some things, which may be hard. This is where finding and facing your dilemma comes in. We'll get there.

To be precise, the general rule of thumb I've adopted is that you can have one project or goal at a time in each of three main life domains: creative work, job work, and personal.

Three projects? That's a lot more than one, yes.

At *most*, you'll have three current projects. But whether that is realistic or not depends on the rest of your life. If you have so many processes running that you are left with only three or four hours of disposable time in a week, stick to one project at a time, and alternate domains as you wrap up one project and free up a bit of time and attention for the next thing.

Creative work

By this, I mean the work that you're doing in a future-building, speculative way. You want to make this work because *you* want to make it. It's possible that it will grow into something that defines future-you. It may or may not make you any money, now or in the future, but that's not what defines it.

Job work

This is the work you do now to support yourself. Whether that means you're a primary caregiver, financially supported by someone else, or you're a freelancer living on client work, or you have a 9-to-5 (or 3-to-midnight, whatever), this is an area that you can address as a stand-alone domain, in which you can build projects to improve your life.

Personal

This is everything else, more or less. Do you want to improve your relationship with your sister? Build a project around it. Do you want to get in shape? Cook dinner every day? These are all projects.

Ambition

One of the reasons Idea Debt is so dangerous is that one of the natural tracks most of us follow when dreaming about our big projects is to imagine how it will be received in the world, and how it will lead to fame and fortune.

Let's get real: Most creative projects don't lead to fame and fortune. This is not a "starving artist" argument. I'm not whining that it's hard to make money with creative work (although it is). I'm stating a fact. Most of the time, creative people make the work, and then they don't do much with it. The "doing something with it" part, by the way, is a new project. It's called marketing and selling.

Here's the thing, though: Most creatives feel like making money with creative work is a requirement for success and thus for the project's worthiness. You've got to be a pro (i.e., get paid for it), or your work is worthless—and this is absolutely untrue. As long as you get what you need out of the work, which may be anything from simply completing it, to sharing it with immediate friends and family, to Beyoncé-level fame (and fortune), the work is a success, and extremely worthwhile.

At the same time, most creative people also feel that the "marketing and selling" project is really icky and overwhelming and scary. I'll be frank: It's a big unknown, few of us get any preparation for it, and it requires learning lots of new skills. I've really enjoyed learning these skills, and this domain is no longer scary and unknown to me, but that's no guarantee you'll feel the same way.

All that said, one way you'll become happier with your creative work is to get really clear on your ambitions for it. If you really do want to sell tons and make a living at it, that will entail very different choices than if you realize that you have to make it but, once it exists, you're fine with sharing it with a much smaller circle, while continuing to make your living some other way.

Maybe once you make the latter realization, you start looking at your "day job" and you create a project to make it a "career" and that eases things up for you. The worst is just not knowing. If you're inchoately wishing for something to be different, feeling frustrated that you're working so hard and things are not falling into place, that's a huge part of what's holding you back.

What do you really want from your creative work?

Is your creative work "simply" an outlet? All creative work is that to some extent: It's meditative and challenging by turns, it stretches our capacities, it brings us to new understandings. It makes us feel better, more whole.

But there's another axis: How many people do you want to communicate with through your work?

Let me explain: If you're a scrapbooker, you're very probably trying to use that creative process to communicate, but the audience may be tiny, just an immediate family circle. If you're Beyoncé, your art is a conduit of communication to (and from) millions upon millions.

I learned to be a very good cook quite young, when most of my friends didn't know how to cook. In college, and for years afterward, I would orchestrate amazing meals: Indian, Italian, Mexican, you name it. I loved to share my food with close friends and even threw a giant party once or twice.

When I fed people, they would often say, "This is so great! Why don't you become a chef?" (Granted, this was partly because I was working such random jobs, and appeared to not know what I wanted from my life...) My response was always, "What? No way. Becoming a chef would put me on a fast track to ruining my love of cooking."

I did a damn good job of identifying where to locate my cooking on my own internal Creation-Communication Matrix, 20 years before I invented the thing.

If you clarify what you really want from your creative work, you can start to make the right decisions about how to move forward with it.

Case in point:

Matt, my husband, is a cartoonist. He's also a talented musician. He's got a musician's ear for the world. He notices motifs in soundtracks, he remembers lyrics, he imagines riffs. For Matt, playing music, thinking about music, and listening to music are all basic requirements for living a good life.

I had a conversation with him a few years ago about his music and his comics.

Comics and activities derived from comics (teaching, editing, translating, workshops, and speaking) are how he makes his living. He's deeply engaged in making his comics and wants to make a big impact with them in the world. I compared that to his music, calling him a "passionate amateur," because he was spending hours every week learning bossa nova songs on his guitar, listening to music, and so on, but seemed not to need to go further than that. I thought that was admirable.

But when I called Matt an "amateur," even in admiration, he got his back up, and that led him to realize that I was wrong: His ambitions for his music were in fact quite a bit larger than our living room. He wanted to be sort of...semi-pro.

And in the ensuing few years, as quixotic as the process sometimes felt—buying the wrong equipment, learning and relearning the software, trying and re-trying to record properly—Matt has gradually trained himself in production and written new songs, and the investment he made shows. He did most of the music for my podcast, he has his own SoundCloud channel*, and he's even got interest from a small label. And who knows, being self-aware as a semi-pro may lead him to decide to become less semi and more pro in the years to come.

If Matt hadn't had that realization, that he really did have a larger goal for the response to his music, he might never have assessed how he actually invested his time and realized that *he had to build the practice that would feed the next version of himself.*

The Creation-Communication Matrix

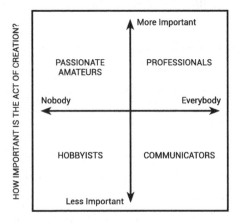

WHO DO YOU WANT TO COMMUNICATE WITH?

HOW IMPORTANT IS THE ACT OF CREATION?

More Important

PASSIONATE AMATEURS

PROFESSIONALS

Nobody

Everybody

HOBBYISTS

COMMUNICATORS

Less Important

* *https://soundcloud.com/mattmadd*

The vertical Y axis on the matrix represents how important the actual act of creation is to you. How serious you are about it? How many hours a week do you want to spend on it? How necessary is it for your sanity and survival? The horizontal X axis represents the intended scope of your audience. On what scale do you want to communicate via your creation? These are both, I should say, extremely personal metrics. No one can (or should) tell you how important creating should be to you, nor what your goals should be for your work.

And, as with Matt, understanding where we are with a given project on the matrix can allow us to consciously decide to move. If we know where we are, we can decide to go somewhere else, and plot a course to actually get there.

In defense of the passionate amateur

If you like to make things, like knitwear or decorative arts, and you've practiced to the point where you're good at it, people are probably always telling you, "you should sell these things!" Perhaps you feel like you should (red flag!)...but you resist ever really trying. You don't really want to. You just like making stuff. If you identify this about yourself correctly, then all you really need to do is figure out how you can sort out a path to get the objects you make out of your workspace so you can feel free to make more of them.

Knowing you're a passionate amateur can bring you an enormous sense of peace. (It also makes it a lot easier to brush off people who push you to do more or go pro, by gifting them with something you've made in order to make space in your house for a new project.)

Are you a passionate amateur singer? You probably spend several nights a week rehearsing with your nonprofessional chorus or opera troupe. Maybe you're a painter? Your main problem is that you probably have more canvases around than you know what to do with. That's a much simpler problem to solve than finding a gallery and going pro.

I love being a passionate amateur gardener. I want nothing more from gardening than to share it with my immediate friends and family. I never want to be paid for it, and I couldn't care less if anyone outside my immediate circle ever sees my garden. If that's you, whether it's about painting, music, crafting, or writing, *own* it. Build your practice for yourself and your small circle. **It's the *practice* of the creative work that's crucial. The communication to the rest of the world is not.**

Creative work doesn't need to earn its keep. If you love what you do, find a way to do more of it.

Teaching in art schools for many years, I saw so many young people coming in who seemed to have decided to go to art school because they liked making art more than most other activities. They decided, "I don't want to go to school for business or math or whatever, so I'll go to art school. I want to make art." I get that, and it makes perfect sense. Making art feeds your soul.

But if you want it to feed your body, too, you've got to move into that top-right quadrant of the matrix, and that entails a whole raft of other activities that are not directly about making art. Do these art students want to go through what it takes to use their art to communicate with the world? Do they really want to professionalize what's essentially an expressive outlet for them? Or do they just think, "I like this so much, I should make it my job?"

Chapter 7

Saying No

**Coming to terms with the necessity of knowing
what your highest priorities are—across all areas of your
life—and aligning what you actually choose
to do with those priorities**

"People think focus means saying yes to the thing you've got to focus on. But that's not what it means at all. It means saying no to the hundred other good ideas that there are. You have to pick carefully. I'm actually as proud of the things we haven't done as the things I have done. Innovation is saying no to 1,000 things." —Steve Jobs

This kind of quote gets tossed around a lot. I'm guessing you've read this one by Steve Jobs, or something like it, before. I'm also guessing you thought about it for a few milliseconds, and possibly thought it was wise, but then forgot it—and certainly never tried to apply it to your own life.

The truth is, saying no to things is incredibly hard. It's only easy to say no to obvious, unappealing time-sucks, but for the other things—the things you would want to say yes to if you weren't bound by the constraints of the time-space continuum—it's not really clear why or how to say no.

Once you really grok this quote, it will sink deep into your soul. But until you do, you're going to be wrestling with yourself over this concept. So let's dive in.

Planning your time with intent

Time is limited. What do you want to do with yours?

You've already got way too much on your plate. You've got a job, you've got friends, possibly a spouse or significant other. You're overdue to call your mom, aren't you? And your kids? Is it possible to ever feel like you spend enough time with them? So what are you doing here?

You're here because you want to make creative work. You can't shake that desire, but maybe you also can't figure out how to make it happen in your already packed life.

Maybe you imagine that because I get a lot of stuff done, I have a simpler life, somehow.

I wish.

In mid-2015, when I was about to launch my book *Out on the Wire*, the podcast based on that book, and a redesigned website, I wrote a blog post to celebrate, called "Cheese and Grapes," wherein I admitted I have a problem with stopping to take a break, or even a breath. It was my secret shame: I beat myself up for not knowing how to chill and take time off to enjoy both the results of the work I'd done and the parts of my life that got less attention while I was doing that work. I told myself, *this* is my problem. I just need to *learn* to stop and relax.

Since then, I've realized that my madness had a real method (though that didn't make it any less mad). I didn't feel I had the option to just stop working, to say no. I have a house and a mortgage, and I have two kids. I'm married to another freelance artist, and we never knew where our income would be coming from a year down the line.

So I said yes.

I always said yes.

I figured out how to fit it in, and told myself that I'll take a break "when things calm down." Sound familiar? When does "crunch time" end?

There are people with good, salaried jobs who have similar issues with cramming too much in and not saying no enough. That may be a separate problem. But when you're a freelance artist in an unstable financial situation (a redundant statement), you can't afford to go around saying no willy-nilly. At least, not when you're an American.

Socialism, capitalism, and workaholism

I lived in France for four years. What struck me in this context was that the French do say no. In fact, sometimes it doesn't even occur to them that yes is an option. It's not that they don't work hard. They do. It's not that they're rolling in dough, either. Quite the contrary.

The French say no, and they stop. Why? There are a lot of reasons, of course, but one major one is that if they fail, they don't have as far to fall. There's a socioeconomic safety net in France, a real one, one that will actually catch you. If you're on public assistance in France, you won't be living comfortably, but you'll live, you'll have housing and healthcare, and your kids will go to daycare for free. Most of the people I know there also live smaller in other ways: They "keep the nut small." If they have to give up on luxuries like a larger car or a big trip in order to take time off, they do it. It's what one does.

I had coffee in Paris with an American children's book author. He had been living there for a while and was about to move home.

I was already starting to think about the things I've been writing about in the last couple of years:

- How do we go about changing the paradigm for creative work?
- How do we make thoughtful choices about our time, make sure the work gets done but also stop and recharge?
- How do we start to address the underlying strategy behind how we make a living at this, so there's not the low-frequency vibration of fear running through everything we do?

The Auteur told me the two things he had started to appreciate most about France as he prepared to leave, which had, when he arrived, been the things that bugged him the most. My first reaction was to laugh. But then I thought for a few minutes, and his insight actually goes pretty deep.

How the French say no

The first thing the Auteur mentioned was the very French attitude of "Not my department." In other words, if a task or problem doesn't fall in your job description, you refuse to take it on. He said, "This drives me insane," but now he sees that it can be really healthy, when used right. What is your work, and what is not your work? Don't say yes to things that are not your job, that you can't handle, and that will drive you nuts. Don't say yes to things that will lead you down the wrong path, to work you don't want or shouldn't be doing.

How the French stop

The second thing the Auteur learned was clocking out. In France, when you're done, you're done. You take a 90-minute lunch break, away from your work desk—and you don't use it to talk about work or have meetings. You leave at six. You work no more than 35 hours a week, even if that means you end up taking a half day on Wednesday. You take your generous vacation weeks every year. (And you take at least two of them during the last two weeks of August.)

You can go to an appliance *superstore* in France at 12:30 p.m. and find it closed for lunch. Bustling businesses shut down *for weeks at a time* for vacation.

These boundaries and limits are frustrating to Americans, who thrive on convenience and are used to constant availability and getting things done when they want to get them done. But the French don't clock out to annoy us.

The Auteur explained it in his trademark way: "All Americans care about is widgets, and all the French care about is fucking." I don't entirely see the French obsession with carnal activity, but maybe I hung out with too many parents of small children.

Another, less vivid way to put it is a saying you may have heard about the French and other Europeans: They work to live, whereas Americans live to work. What the French do care about is personal life, family life, and the division between that and work. Americans could learn from this.

However, as I said above, while it's true that Americans are always looking for efficiency, for those of us who are self-employed (or un- or under-employed), making our lives function financially is completely on us, and that's scary as shit.

Yes, I'd tell myself that I was a stupid workaholic and no one on their deathbed moans with regret, wishing they'd *worked* more, but that knowledge never caused me to slow down or make other choices.

Without pulling back and reworking the whole paradigm, the only way I made a reasonable living was to just keep cramming more low-paid work into the same few hours. That's why I chased widget-making, not for the love of the widgets themselves.

Pull back and rework the whole paradigm

If I'd thought things through more clearly in terms of what work I wanted to be doing day to day, and what I wanted that work to do in the world—if I'd invented the Creation-Communication Matrix years ago, in other words—I could have said no to lots of things. Things I should have said no to. And in doing so, I'd have been freed up to say yes to other things that, in retrospect, were probably more important.

Instead, I fell into the Busy Trap, adding more and more onto my plate until I was completely burned out. I'm still trying to dig out of that trap, but I'm halfway there. I can see that there's a way, despite having two kids, a house, a full-time job, and a full-on creative career. I can do all that and not be "busy." Which is absolutely *not* to say that I can do *everything*. Doing all that I do means saying no to about a billion things I wish I could say yes to.

That is the dilemma I face. I've made some very hard choices to prioritize my creative work over other things. Sometimes, I make the wrong choices. *But mostly, they're just choices I wish I didn't have to make.*

When I was a teen and in my 20s, music was at the center of my life. I went to rock shows multiple times a week and went dancing as often as possible. I was in a band. When I met Matt, who likes music even more than I do and plays much better, I started unconsciously "delegating" music to him, to the point where music takes up a tiny fraction of my consciousness now.

- I used to garden more and build things. Now I have children.
- I used to cook elaborate meals. Now I cook simply, although that's partly due to the tastes of the aforementioned children.
- I used to try to learn about wine but now have "delegated" that knowledge to Matt as well.

The olden days. 2008. Sigh.

Some of these things will be making a roaring comeback in future years as my kids get older and develop outside lives of their own. Just not right now. Now, it's NO.

Please understand, I do not mean to say that if you're a single parent of three who is holding down two jobs, that you and I have the same issues. Clearly, you will have less time available for creative work than I will. I don't want to minimize that. That's real.

But what that means is that whatever time you *do* have available for creative work, even if it's only 10 minutes a day, or 30 minutes a week, that time is so valuable to you, it's so precious, that you've got to make the smartest, most conscious choices possible.

Saying no to other people

Time constraints are not the only reason saying no is hard. By its nature, "no" is an answer to a question, and that question is, "Will you do X?" Sometimes the person asking is yourself, and then the job is to figure out what your real priorities are and if this project aligns. No biggie, right?

But often the request is coming from a real, other person. And then you will face possible...conflict. It sounds funny to put it that way, but confrontation is tough for anyone and can approach phobia status for some people. Here's the thing, though. If you do X, and resent doing it, you and the asker will both be aware of that at a more or less subliminal level. You will damage your relationship with the person by doing it as much as by not doing it. Let me just repeat what I hope your BFF or your mom is always telling you: Be honest, and be quick about it. Don't leave things hanging, so the person wonders whether you'll do it or not, or sometime in the future, or whatever. A "no" is way better than a "maybe." A "maybe" drags everything out and prevents the other person from moving on to find some other way to get the thing done.

Stop being "nice"

You do a lot of the things you do so that you'll look good to a peer group and therefore be known as being nice or cool. Examples abound: Working late when you're overtired and basically useless. Baking four dozen cupcakes with individual decorations every single time there's a bake sale. Doing comics or illustration for free for a friend's fanzine. Putting up an elaborate light display for the holidays.

Some projects in this category are also things you really care about. Perhaps your whole neighborhood goes all out on light displays, and that's a huge source of pride and enjoyment to you. Maybe you really love that fanzine and want to be a part of it. I'm not telling you to quit this whole category of "yeses" just because they also serve the purpose of making you look good. I'm just saying, separate those threads and be aware of them. Remember you can't do everything. Learn to say no when no is what's called for.

Saying no to yourself

Saying no to yourself is all about ridding yourself of Idea Debt so that you're unencumbered enough to be able to say YES in ways that align with your priorities. In Chapter 2, you took the first step toward doing that by taking an Idea Debt Inventory, and we'll be getting back to your Idea Debt list at the end of this chapter.

In the next chapter, we'll build on those previous activities by learning how to evaluate and prioritize that Idea Debt list, an activity that will enable you to determine what you really want (i.e., saying YES). Once you are clear on what you want, saying no to yourself will come down to two things: fear of losing income (as I discussed above), and sunk costs.

Sunk costs

We started talking about the Sunk Costs Fallacy back in Chapter 2: Drowning in Idea Debt. That is where you will need to be most on guard for how Sunk Costs will distort your decision-making. According to Wikipedia, "a sunk cost is a cost that has already been incurred and cannot be recovered." In other words, all that time you spent dreaming about the project that has not materialized is a sunk cost. If you started making notes for your comic, sunk cost. If you're on the third draft of your screenplay, whoa. Hello, sunk costs. You've devoted ten years to the pursuit of a career in 3D animation? My *lord*, that's a lot of sunk costs!

Now, when I say "sunk costs," I'm not telling you that any of those projects I just called out are *not* worth pursuing. Maybe they are. But the nature of sunk costs is that they are unrecoverable. Nothing you do will bring back the time and effort you've already invested. In other words, sunk costs may not be time wasted per se, but they are always time spent. And you can't change that.

But you do have control over the time spent in the future. So if you allow your sunk costs to be the deciding factor in whether you *continue* on a project or not, you're falling for the Sunk Costs Fallacy.

Let's take our hypothetical 3D animator. If she's spent ten years in the field and worked diligently, she'll have some reputation, some connections, she'll have skills. The dilemma is that she's discovered her true love is being outside and working with plants, and she wants to work in landscape design. Creating animation entails being inside staring at a screen for eight to twelve hours a day. If she's decided that she's not heading somewhere she wants to be, then the only choice is to change gears and do something else with her time, a new direction and time allocation that aligns with who and where she wants to be in the future. It will be painful, yes, and she should allow herself to mourn a little. As should you when you're in a similar dilemma.

But what's more painful, doing this after ten more years? Or after 15? Or, god forbid, on your deathbed? Do not let your past decisions and past investments dictate your future actions.

How to know when "no" is your best option

I've said over and over again: Real lives are complicated, *and* that fact does not exclude you from being able to make your work. However. Among all the processes you do every week and all the projects you take on are very likely many things that you don't really want to be doing. In fact, you may not have even decided to do them. You just find yourself in the middle of a life full of stuff and wonder, "How did I get here?" As hard as it is to do, you must get some distance on that morass and ask yourself, "Is this how I want to run my life? Are these things what I choose?" Figuring out the answers to these questions is how you shift your mindset and decide whether and how to do whatever you do with conscious intent.

I subscribe to the newsletter of the amazing Kelly Diels, who writes about feminism, time, and how that should inform business (and by extension, any project). A few months ago, she sent out a newsletter that kind of blew the top of my head off and made the costs of all my yes and no choices concrete and real:

> *So many of the things that were normal goods and services in schools when I was growing up are now considered by school boards to be luxuries. And where the budgets end, parents start organizing, fundraising, volunteering.*

> *And by parents, I mean mostly mothers and women (at least in my kids' schools).*

> *Now, I don't want to suggest we shouldn't be invested in our schools or we shouldn't be present and involved with our children, their educators, and their education.*

> *What I do want to draw attention to is this: **When governments and school boards cut dollars from their budgets, we step in with our uncompensated labor to fill the gap. The revenue and dollar value of our off-the-books time and labor is real, and really valuable, but it is not a line item in these official budgets.***

So most of us are philanthropists. With our time. Whether we want to be or not...

...So then I started thinking about all the places in which I am a time-philanthropist. What if I applied an hourly rate to that? How much am I actually contributing?

Again: it's cool to volunteer, with love, and when and where you consciously and explicitly want to volunteer to support causes you care about. **But I have zero desire to continue cosigning inequitable systems or unprotested problems with my unconscious contributions and my uncompensated time.**

I want to draw attention to the systemic nature of what scholar Diane Negra calls "women's chronic temporal crisis." I also want to shift my personal practices so that I actually have personal practices. I want to account for the way I'm contributing my time to the economy and The System. I want a number.

Because if The Economy was a person and said to me, Hey Kelly, this year I'm going to need $24,000 from you to keep my unjust mechanisms working smoothly, I'd be like, hell no.

What institutions—like corporations and governments—are only able to function effectively because of our free labor?"

Whoa. I mean, whoa. *Yes.*

Diels extends this understanding not just to institutions but to families, to friendships, to business relationships, to clients, you name it. The key phrase in all of this is: "it's cool to volunteer, with love, and when and where you *consciously and explicitly* want to volunteer." (Emphasis mine.) Externalize it, make it concrete, and *decide*.

Although Diels's focus is on how this principle affects women's lives—and, let's be real, as a general rule, it's a much bigger problem for women—the exact same idea applies to everyone's lives: How many tasks or roles are you "volunteering" for that you didn't even realize were choices, much less decide consciously to do them?

Time-pricing and time-tithing

Diels addressed how to assess your time choices in a bracingly practical exercise, using concepts she called "Time-pricing" and "Time-tithing."

She assigned a dollar value to her hours, based on her professional hourly rate (time-pricing).

Then she decided how many dollars/hours she would "gladly and consciously" donate this month, and to what—her community, her family, schools and extracurriculars, causes, etc.

Then, she tracked her time. Using her time-tracking records, she assigned a dollar value to each of the things she'd spent time on.

In the process of assessing all this, Diels decided how she felt about what it revealed to her. She quit fighting with a person. She decided to pay for more caregiver time to help with her kids. She said yes to school board meetings: It was worth it. She felt great about herself, knowing how much time and help she was giving to people and organizations she loved.

Activity: Time-pricing

Find this activity and any relevant worksheets in the Growing Gills Workbook at http://jessicaabel.com/gg-reader.

Materials: Trot out your time-tracking inventory. The time-tracking you've been doing will come in handy again later in this chapter, but here you can use it to make a tally of what time you're spending on which activities and people.

Step 1: Give your time a value—it doesn't have to be dollars, but that helps make things pretty stark—and do the math to calculate how much you're donating to specific activities and people. Questions to consider might include:

- How much time are you "donating" to fighting with someone at work?
- Are you happy with your time-philanthropy?
- What do you want to do less of?
- What do you want to do more of?

Step 2: Take note of your realizations based on your time-pricing, and use your assessments to set intentions for the coming week. For example, knowing that doing some project will be the equivalent of donating $500 to that person or organization makes the choice a lot clearer!

(You may also have a partner or roommate who needs to also time-track, time-price, and time-tithe to bring some equity to your relationship and to shared household projects and tasks. That's a tough conversation, but maybe this documentation will help you have it.)

Chapter 8

Saying YES

Choosing your highest creative priority, and saying yes to finishing

S aying yes is just as important as saying no.

You need clarity to say yes. You need to know what matters to you, and what criteria to use to decide.

But finally, you need to say yes to what matters, and embrace that yes, and make it real.

I know you'll have doubts. That's completely normal. But coming to trust yourself and your taste, and to believe that you're worth it, that's key.

It's all about connecting the you of today to the you of the future. Will future-you be happy that you took on this project and finished it? How will it change things for future-you?

If you have trouble connecting to this future self—and most of us do—here's a little trick I learned: run a picture of yourself through one of those virtual-aging image generators (Google "aging image generator" or "image aging app" and you'll find something), and think about his or her life. In a podcast interview, the writer AJ Jacobs, who does all kinds of life-hacking experiments, said he has his aged face come up on a screen saver every once in a while, just to jolt his awareness and prompt him to re-evaluate himself. I'm thinking about trying that myself.

Whatever catalyst you use, the upshot is, self-control is all about empathy for future-you.

Learning to honor your personal goals

My student Michael Wittmann had "always done some art on the side" of his demanding full-time job as a lawyer for the Austrian government. To be clear, for him "art on the side" meant three European-style comics albums, 13 years of weekly illustrations for the long-running sci-fi novel series *Perry Rhodan*, short strips, and caricatures. He's no Sunday painter.

Yet even Michael, who had juggled a serious professional art career alongside a very nontrivial day job, felt completely out of control when it came to his personal work.

I always knew I needed to do some art, because when I don't do art for a long time, I get depressed. And that's not good.

When I know somebody is waiting to get my work and there is a deadline, I always deliver on time. But when I try to do some personal work, it hardly ever gets beyond the development stage.

I lose excitement, I get bogged down with research, I get distracted, and some other project seems so much more exciting. Then a commission comes along and I am completely focused on it. All thoughts about the personal projects disappear.

Sometime after I have completed the commission work, I remember something about my earlier plans, leaf through my notes and sketches. Sometimes I can get some of the excitement back and the cycle repeats, sometimes I just file the notes and sketches away for later completion, which probably never happens.

When Perry Rhodan didn't give me any more commissions, I kind of fell into a big black hole. I felt desperate. I would not produce anything without an external deadline. And even with a deadline I usually did not manage to finish anything more complex than illustrations or single-page comics or cartoons. For years I have aborted all projects of multi-page comic stories.

I had to give myself some structure, some deadlines like I'd been used to, and I didn't know how.

So when he came to the Creative Focus Workshop, his aims were really quite modest. He simply wanted "to learn to be as dependable and productive for my own creative work as I am when somebody else gives me an assignment and a deadline. To learn how to keep a schedule I set myself." ✗

Yet finding a way to be self-motivated and pursue goals that no one is imposing from the outside is one of the hardest things we do as creative people. To commit to doing work purely because you want to is a profound statement of trust in yourself and your judgment. It means you have to get way out on the wire. You have to say a definitive *yes* to yourself.

Michael's One Goal for the Creative Focus Workshop was to complete "Rotkäppchen"—a 10-page version of the Little Red Riding Hood story—done in a classic Jack "King of Comics" Kirby style.

Last spring, I read more than 100 issues of Erik Larsen's Savage Dragon *[itself inspired by Kirby]. It made me wish to do my own Jack Kirby homage. And then I heard that the next anthology of Viennese comic book artists would be on the theme of fairy tales.*

In the midst of work on his project, Michael wrote his thanks to the Creative Focus Workshop community for helping him make progress toward his goal.

Yesterday I did some character sketches, bits and pieces of dialogue, narration, and panel designs for my Little-Red-Riding-Hood-as-a-Jack-Kirby-homage project, and, as usual, my mind started to tell me how silly this whole project was, that I will make a fool of myself, that I am not good enough to draw a decent Kirby imitation anyway and any other project on my Idea Debt list would be so much more worthwhile than this one.

Three weeks ago this would have stopped me, but thanks to the Workshop I could take it as a good thing and just continue my work.

Amazing! I feel so powerful at this moment, it is unbelievable.

Reader, he finished it. "Rotkäppchen" was published in the anthology "Fairy Tales," published by the Viennese Comic Artists community "Tisch 14."

How I spend my days is how I spend my life

Work, even work you love, is a means to an end, and that end is your life. You work in order to live your life. Both to pay for your life, and to add meaning to your life. But it's part of the bigger picture. It's subordinate to your life, even if you love your work. Take vacations, stop for lunch, stop at the end of the day and spend time with people you love.

I'm not a slogan-clipper, but one that I wrote down and stuck to my drawing table is "How we spend our days is, of course, how we spend our lives," from *The Writing Life* by Annie Dillard.

One of the things that drove me to choose the path of writing about how we build a creative life in the real world is the fact that every single time I talked to others in my field, we asked one another: "How do you make it work?" The undercurrent being, always: "I must be doing something wrong, right? Because this just isn't sustainable. You seem like you're making it. What's your secret?"

The "secret," unfortunately, mostly turned out to be: Just keep hacking away at the same stuff, do more and more, and try not to think about whether this will still be enough a year from now, or ten years. Most of us fool ourselves into thinking that our current state of being is just a temporary situation, that once this next big push is over, things will get easier.

The fantasy is that the grass will be much greener in some outcome-contingent future: Once we get some contract, get picked up by a publisher, kickstart a book, sell a painting, meet some director, get a part, or whatever...there will be a change, we'll feel different, and we'll relax a bit.

If you find yourself in this trap, it's not your fault. This is the myth society feeds us about following our passions. We think that if we get good enough at what we do, someone with enough power, money, and influence to make a change in our lives will find us, lift us out of the grind, and change the playing field.

That's just not how it works. The fact that has happened for two or three people you can think of isn't meaningful. That's the anomalous exception rather than the rule, the artistic equivalent to winning the lottery. You can and must take control of your own decisions and work, and you must make it happen. You can. This is how:

- Get clarity on what it is that you're intending to do, and whether you're actually doing it.
- Make smart choices about where to devote your time and energy. Say yes.
- Make a strategic plan to move, quickly, in the right direction.

If you feel overwhelmed and blocked and slightly crazed trying to make your creative life work, believe me: You are not alone, and it's not your fault. Most important, with mindful attention, you can make it better.

How you spend your days is how you spend your life.

Idea Debt, step 2:
One Goal to Rule Them All

We're all on the same page: You need to focus on one creative goal at a time. You realize this doesn't mean quitting every other priority in your life. You've decided what role you want your creative work to play in your life. You're braced to say no and to say yes.

But no to what? And more important, *yes* to what? This is the tough part, actually choosing. What you need is a sieve: You need a tool that will help you understand your choices and figure out how to spend your time.

You've probably made a million lists of stuff you really, really want to do in your life. What makes this list any different? Well, this time, you're going to get really clear on **why** you want to do one project versus another. How does it fit into the big picture? This is not necessarily about deciding definitively, forever; it's more about what's the right project for NOW. **It's about prioritizing.**

What you're going to do is choose One Goal that you will pursue for the next 6 to 12 weeks. If the overall project you want to devote yourself to is bigger in scope than that, you'll choose one sub-project that you can finish and check off in this specific, and short, span of time. The idea is, as you get better at building your creative work into your life, you need to choose projects that you can envision in their entirety.

Activity:
Choose one goal

**Find this activity and any relevant worksheets
in the Growing Gills Workbook at http://jessicaabel.com/gg-reader.**

Step 1. Get out your Idea Debt worksheet, and make notes on each of your ideas to categorize them according to four specific criteria that will help you to prioritize and focus: Quick Wins, Follow the Money, Platform-Building, and Big Picture.

Four Criteria

1. Quick Wins. If you're struggling with finishing projects at all, you've got to pick a quick win. Can you finish this project pretty quickly and get it out into the world while you turn to new things? Then it's a quick win. Getting smaller things done will build your skill set and your confidence so you can set more ambitious, longer-term goals for later. By the way, if this is your situation and your list doesn't contain any projects that offer you quick wins, that's a red flag. Come up with some.

Definitions of Quick Wins:

- You've got the project 90% done; you just have to buckle down and wrap it up.
- The project is really small, but getting it off your plate would be helpful in clearing your mental space.

2. Follow the Money. If your creative work is your job, money is the goal. Not because you're a money-grubbing capitalist, but because you've got to put a chicken in your pot. Additionally, even if this is *not* how you earn your keep, making money for what you do is important: money is your energy and time crystalized. You invest your energy into your work, and when someone pays you for it, that's like putting your time and energy into a battery, storing it to use and give you time or energy when you need it. Is there a way you can make money from this project as a direct result of your actions?

Definitions of Follow the Money:

- You know an editor who will pay you to publish your article or a producer who would seriously consider paying you to run your audio piece on the radio.
- You can access public spaces and forums at which you can sell your work to target audiences.
  Examples:
  > You can sell your artwork at an upcoming fair.
  > You're planning to self-publish your comic and can buy a table at a convention at which you can sell it.

Note that "follow the money" is not wishful or magical thinking. Thinking "this will be so awesome it will get optioned by a movie producer" or "it's sure to be a bestseller" does not meet the "follow the money" criteria. "Follow the money" is about tangible ways to earn money from your work that you can affect with your own direct action.

3. Platform-Building. This category intersects with all the others, but sometimes you can see how a particular project will be better at building bridges for you—with colleagues, influencers, your audience, or all of the above. Will finishing this project have a direct effect on building your network or audience? Then it's a platform-building project.

Definitions of Platform-Building:

- You know editors or producers to whom you can submit work.
- You are starting a podcast or blog.
- You can make minicomics and trade them with other cartoonists or give them to editors.
- The project is something for which your existing audience has been clamoring.

4. Big Picture. If you've already shown yourself that you can really finish projects, and you've built the stamina to stick with it even when you don't have the reassurance that comes from quick wins, you can challenge yourself to ask longer-term questions: *Where do I want to be in five years? And which project is the path to that future self?* Does this project represent the *next big step* for you? (NOTE: We will come back to this item at the end of the book, so if this is too scary to contemplate now, don't. You'll feel more equipped to do it later.)

Definitions of Big Picture:

- Is the project something you'll look back on five years from now and be glad you did? The key here is whether the project represents a leap in growth, so you look back afterward and think, "wow, that really was a turning point in my new _____" (as opposed to "welp, got that off my plate").
- Does the project build the next step in your career or creative ambitions, even if it's not in line with what you're doing right now?
- Is this project taking you toward where you see yourself in the future?
- Is the project going to be really hard, but you know it's the right thing to do?

5. Bonus Criterion: Does this project represent something someone else wants you to do, but you don't, really? Example goal: Get into Harvard. Is this your goal? Or your parents'? This is not actually a Bonus Criterion. It's a Bogus Criterion. If it's not _your_ goal, don't do it.

Step 2. Once you've evaluated your projects by the four criteria, carry it around in your pocket until you're almost ready to work on the next chapter. When you turn your focus to a topic like "what are all my projects, and why are they important to me?" your brain will be working on it day and night. So when you wake up in the morning, take notes on what you're thinking. On your commute, don't listen to a podcast, just think. Don't bring your smartphone to the bathroom, bring your list. Think about it in the shower. Think about it when you're cooking.

Create space in your life to let yourself ponder for a couple of days.

Step 3. Sometime before you dive into Chapter 9, take a hard look at your list and do two things:

- Cross off, and delete as fully as you can from your brain, all the projects that don't line up with your creative goals, including:
  > things other people want you to do that you don't;
  > things you thought you wanted to do, but on review, they don't motivate you;
  > things you feel like you "should" do. Monsters not allowed here.

- Do a final gut-check. You've done the work to think through whether the project has confidence-building, financial, audience-building, or body-of-work-building potential. But really, truly: How do you feel when you think about each project? (Marie Kondo would ask: "Does it spark joy?") "Hold" each idea in your hands and immerse yourself in it. Creative work is absolutely not joyful all the time. But if the basic concept of doing this activity or making this thing doesn't spark joy, even before you've started, ask yourself: Why the hell are you still trying to do it?

Remember, you may be holding on to ideas that represent a past moment in your life when they excited you and represented what you wanted then, but they no longer resonate, nor do they represent where you want to go.

These ideas constitute your "attachment to the past" category (Idea Debt Type N). There's nothing wrong with wanting to retain this memory. If you want to do so, write down what you remember, what you think of when you consider this idea, then archive and file that paper in an "Old Ideas" folder. If you acknowledge how important they were to you, you can let them go and bid them a definitive goodbye.

Step 4. Using the criteria of quick wins, money, relationship-building, and big-picture alignment with your vision of where you want to go with your creative work, **pick a project or phase of a project you want to devote your creative energy to next.** Make it something you can finish, or mark a major milestone on, in a period of 6 to 12 weeks. Achieving milestones is a way to build up your confidence that *you are a finisher*.

If you still can't decide based on the criteria assessments you have, close your eyes, spin around, and point to something. Seriously. The most important thing you can do here is CHOOSE. Choose and move forward.

Some examples of excellent goals with a 6- to 12-week scope:

- Finish your first podcast episode.
- Plan and launch a new blog.
- Outline your book.
- Get an alpha of your app written and out to testers.
- Draw chapter one of your already scripted graphic novel.
- Rehearse and mount a singing recital.
- Create a solid writing routine. (Yes, goals can be meta in that way.)

Step 5. Write your 6- to 12-week goal on a separate piece of paper. (Feel free to embellish with stars and lightning bolts.) Then write down *how you will define having achieved this goal*.

Step 6. (Optional) Post your one goal on Facebook or Instagram with the hashtags #onegoal and #growinggills. Let us help you celebrate your intention! I can't wait to see what you'll do.

Once you set this goal, you may find yourself feeling energized, wanting to work on it right away. DO IT. Even if you don't have your system all set up yet, use this energy to launch you into action.

Remember: Friends can help you figure out what makes the most sense. But in the end, YOU have to be the one to make, and commit to, this decision. No one can force you.

You're doing this because your creative work is central to who you are. You're hesitating because it's scary to commit. It is hard, but it's necessary.

Make it so.

Put your other beloved ideas on hold—for now

For the rest, the ideas you love but you're putting on hold but hope to come back to, you know how this works: You will be tempted to pick them up again as soon as the going gets tough with project No. 1. So let's do a little ceremony that will help your brain and heart fully process this decision you've taken.

Fold up your Idea Debt Inventory like this: It doesn't have to look beautiful. It just needs to stay closed.

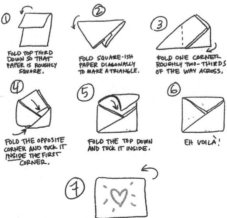

⭐ Tell your postponed projects that you love them, and you just need some space. Draw a heart on this little packet, and place it on the top shelf of your bedroom closet. Not your studio/office/workroom closet, your *bedroom* closet. If you work in your bedroom, don't quibble. Follow the spirit, not the letter, of this assignment, and put it somewhere away from your working area, in a safe spot.

If you've got physical notes or peripheral materials pertaining to the projects you're shelving, get literal about it: Put them in a shoebox on the shelf in your closet.

Close the closet.

Those projects and ideas will still be there in six to 12 weeks when you're done with the project you chose as your one goal for now.

Choose your tool

I've mentioned the idea of a "system," a powered exoskeleton that will enhance your abilities and support your weak spots when it comes to completing your projects. Sounds incredible, right?

What does this look like in practice? Unfortunately, it is not anything near as cool as Sigourney Weaver got to wield in *Aliens*. In practice, it looks like an app, or a notebook. Sorry. I know that's disappointing. Maybe draw a robot on the cover?

What this system does, though, is kind of magic. It essentially serves as an external hard drive for your brain. That's techy and cool, right? Your system is where you put all the churning anxiety, all the lists, all the planning, so that it doesn't live in your mind. You can even put your Should Monster in there if it will help.

From here on, your job will be to put everything you want to do, every flitting open loop, every plan for your big creative project, in your system. And it needs to be ONE system. If you start leaving little bits of your life in other places, in notepads and on matchbooks, you leave a little bit of attention with each of those things, and soon you're back to this sense of generalized anxiety that you're losing track of stuff (because without constant vigilance and re-remembering, you are). You need to know, when you boot up that hard drive, that you'll find everything you need. If you aren't confident of that, you won't trust it. And if you don't trust it, you won't download your brain into it and enjoy some much-needed peace.

You're going to be tempted to spend days messing around with different options. But let's get one thing straight: *The specific tool isn't all that important.* If you start falling down a Google rabbit hole, time to quit it and use a low-tech and unpretty, yet effective, legal pad.

The point is not the tool, but USING the tool, and building a reliable system.

Reliable means:

- You will use it, daily, many times a day.
- You will put *everything* in this same place so that when you look for it, you'll find it.
- You will review it regularly. (We'll do this in Chapter 14.)

You've got to get everything in there, and you've got to LOOK AT IT.

Too many systems (in other words, places to keep to-dos and notes) = no systems.

The point of a system is to *replace your memory*. The only thing you have to remember is: *Use the system*.

But: If you get too caught up in building the system and filling it with tasks, it's self-defeating. Your creative practice is about feeling at one with your work. And there's no way you're doing that if you find yourself mired in the system. If setting up task lists stops you, or if you drop your system entirely, you're worse off than if you never started—you've lost that time. Meanwhile, if you have a half-assed system, but you **use** it, you're better off.

I'm not advocating going all half-assed. No. I'm all about complete, whole asses. But the point is not to force you into a box, it's to build a support system that works for you.

Activity:
Choose your tool

Find this activity and any relevant worksheets
in the Growing Gills Workbook at http://jessicaabel.com/gg-reader.

Step 1. Pick a tool. Pick any one that appeals to you. Don't spend more than a half hour or so on each, testing. You can always switch if you need to.

Step 2. In your tool, create a project header for your big project, or title a notebook page. We'll do more on this in the next chapter, so just leave it at that for now.

Step 3. Create projects (or pages in your notebook) for other categories of open loops in your life, in any way that makes sense. Examples: Teaching, by class, and teaching admin. Family, by person, or all together. Short-term projects like moving or taxes. (Taxes can be set up as repeating projects in most digital systems...unfortunately.)

Step 4. Enter your open loops' tasks under those projects, with due dates where called for. If you're using a paper system, you may want one page devoted to all tasks with concretely short deadlines (this week). Electronically, you might tag all such tasks "this week."

Chapter 9

The Black Box

Breaking down giant, scary projects into small, achievable steps

You've picked your One Goal and said good riddance to Idea Debt. You've cleaned your desk and done a full Brain Download. You feel fresh, renewed. Ready to work. You sit down to get started and...anxiety crawls up your spine. Before you know it, you're on Facebook. Or playing a video game. Or vacuuming, for god's sake.

Why can't you just freaking focus already?

Does this mean you're a lost cause, that you're not cut out for doing creative work? Absolutely not. It just means you don't know your next step.

Procrastination is tied to anxiety. It causes anxiety, but *it is also caused by anxiety*. This anxiety stems from not having thought through the steps, the literal actions, that will get you to your goal. In fact, you may not actually know what all the steps are. That's part of the problem with creative work. Sometimes the work consists of "think about this thing for a while." And that's super vague and unhelpful, not to mention something most of us are amazingly bad at doing under the best of circumstances. (Note: Our world of digital devices clamoring for our attention 24-7-365 is definitely not the best of circumstances.)

When I'm in the flow of doing creative work, to some extent I lose my sense of my physical self. I feel deeply connected to what I'm doing, and time slips by. That doesn't mean I'm necessarily doing excellent work; it just means that one thought or action leads to the next in a natural way—I know where I'm headed, so I never have to focus on the path.

By contrast, when I don't have a plan or know what my next steps are, that's when sitting down to work feels like gazing into the void. I sense that all the pieces I need to pin down are floating around me, just out of reach, and my anxiety rises. I almost literally feel this pressure in my throat, my center of gravity rising—the opposite of the rooted feeling I get from being in the flow.

At that point, it's a hell of a lot easier to go fold laundry than it is to sit with my anxiety.

That's procrastination.

Anxiety is energy without a path

Anxiety is energy with no place to go. Keyword: energy. You want to act. You have that energy in you. You just have to tap it.

To tap it, you have to create a *path* for it to flow through.

We spend so much time thinking about the end result we desire (e.g. "I have a published book!") that we completely fail to work out all the steps that will get us there, then to put them on a calendar, and then, step by step, to get them done. So time passes, and no book is made.

Cartoonist Michi Mathias, a student in my Creative Focus Workshop, came to me with her version of this common situation. She felt really burned by her attempts to work on her big projects. She'd tried all kinds of tricks, but nothing seemed to work:

If I schedule slots in my diary, I manage to forget/ignore them; I've created a detailed notebook with the Get Things Done approach and then never looked at it. I'd even joined a 100-day online program on Facebook earlier this year and chosen one of those projects as my goal, but it wasn't enough just to receive encouragement to keep working on it every day. This is just to say why I'm somewhat hesitant about more programs, as I seem to be strangely resistant.

I asked Michi what her work process had looked like before she started the Creative Focus Workshop. Her response: "Ha! Process? I would come up with drafts, but not get much further, unless [it was] for paid commissions, in which case they would get done because there was a deadline."

This incredibly common problem stems from feeling obligations to other people more deeply than to yourself. Your dilemma is: What will it take to honor my own needs as highly as other people's?

You're not broken; you're facing the unknown

If and when you procrastinate, it is not because you're broken. It's because you're facing unknowns. Once you figure out what those unknowns are, and what questions you need to answer, you'll start moving forward.

Creative person, brace yourself: Each new project you start will bring you to this place where you want to procrastinate, because you will have questions you haven't answered, questions you don't even know to ask. And that will cause you anxiety. But if you let yourself gaze into the Black Box and allow yourself to think about it, you'll find the questions. And eventually, the process of working through them will bring you to the answers.

If you know you're approaching the Black Box and that you're going to feel anxious, you'll be braced for it, and you'll be able to get through it. More to the point, you can be prepared for this stage with tools and techniques that will reduce the pain of the unknowns.

But it takes time. It takes slowing down and allowing yourself to stew, to sit with the anxiety and let it happen. Having a plan for how to work through it—and helping you create this plan is the central objective of this chapter—will make getting through the discomfort of that phase of the creative process more possible. But you still have to choose not to fold the laundry instead.

As of today, Michi has completed and published two projects, one of them a 44-page self-published book she'd been mulling over for at least 15 years. Here's how she pulled it off:

> *That breaking-down stuff is really good. In fact, one of the pages in my journal was breaking down the book. I figured out when it had to go to the printer. I figured out I had to do about 10 pages a month, so that gave me an idea of how much I had to do by day. That was really useful, sort of like a mind map or...a flow chart. I like flow charts. Breaking the book down to steps, and thinking through when the steps have to be done to get to the goal was really really useful.*

Michi still lives with more unknowns in her schedule than you might guess. She's never going to be militaristic in her approach to her system. That's what makes it uniquely hers. But committing to all that "breaking-down stuff" gave Michi a sense of control over her own life and decisions. She no longer felt victimized by her Pressing to-dos or random impulses because she realized she could *decide* what to devote her attention to:

> *I don't have a schedule, I can't define how much time I have. But nevertheless, something's happened. These Idea Debt objects just sat on the shelf, for years, collecting dust. Until—I guess it's just a change of mindset—believing it's possible. Just deciding, "Yes, I will actually do it."*

That's the "conscious" part of conscious decision. If you've got a project plan for how to get from here to there, if you've drawn a roadmap, you can focus on the next tiny, achievable step. Once you put your foot on that path, the sense of accomplishment you have as you check things off your list gradually leads you to believe that you're actually capable of finishing the project you envision. (Which you are.)

Michael Wittmann, whom we met back in Chapter 8 saying a powerful *Yes* to his long-form comics goals, felt that his biggest takeaway from the Creative Focus Workshop was laying out a project over time, breaking it down to stages, and then tracking weekly (which we'll get to in Chapter 15, Planning Backward)

It's great: I know exactly what to do in the time I want to spend on making art. There's always something specific to do. You don't have to wonder and get lost in it.

In the past, when I got more intensely into one project, and it started to feel like work, very quickly other ideas would come up which seemed so much more exciting, and so I didn't get anything done.

This system with the Bullet Journal [a paper-based tool to track your progress and goals] and the six-week tracking—it gives me a direction.

The fact that you end up on Facebook doesn't mean you're "a procrastinator." It means that you have a vision for where you want to arrive with your big creative project in, like, two, three, or five years, but you don't know what the daily work you need to do to get there actually looks like.

If you have a system for how to go about working, and you know what questions to ask, how to break down a larger task into smaller pieces, then you grant yourself control over your creative practice.

Take control of the path

If you did the Stuff Audit Activity (in Chapter 3: Open Loops) you will have a frighteningly long list of things to do, many with deadlines, some of them Pressing. Have you gotten traction on those things? No?

I can tell you why, without even knowing what they are: You don't know your next action.

What I'm about to say applies as much to mundane items on your list like "get a flu shot" as it does to things like "launch my podcast":

Those are not actions. They are projects.

The project is the forest (sometimes a very Dark Forest, which we'll explore in greater depth in Chapter 17) and actions are the trees. **Projects are things we want or need to get done that involve multiple steps.**

Even something as simple as a phone call—"call Aunt Betty"—can be a project with a series of hidden steps if you don't have her new phone number or you don't know when she gets back from vacation, which adds "call mom to get Aunt Betty's number" or "check email to see what Aunt Betty told me about her vacation" to your list of actions to get to completion. If you've been not-calling Aunt Betty, these hidden actions may hold the secret to why. On the other hand, Aunt Betty might be really annoying. Also a dilemma!

My point with the above example isn't to overcomplicate or add anxiety to the more ordinary life projects. It's to put into sharp relief that if even familiar things that seem small in scope turn out, upon close inspection, to involve multiple steps, it's no wonder that new creative projects are so challenging to get off the ground and stick with to completion. A project like a novel, a podcast, a comic book, a blog, a startup software company? Oh, man. Those goals contain so many hidden actions. There are actions inside actions.

But you *can* take control of even the largest projects. Here's what you will do:

1. Take your big project and break it down into action steps. (Easier said than done, I know. Help follows in this chapter via the two Activities.)
2. Put the steps into a tracking system. (We will get to this in the last activity in this chapter.)
3. Schedule the actions that lead to leaping, or even inching, your project forward on your calendar (Chapter 10).
4. Review your system, on a regular basis, at a minimum weekly (Chapter 14). Sounds simple. It is, in fact, simple. That's the point.

It's simple...but it's not easy.

You might be tempted to skip it, or skimp on it at least. Don't. These simple four steps are unreasonably hard, but shockingly valuable when done right.

Activity:
Break down a project into actions,
Part 1: Ask all the questions

**Find this activity and any relevant worksheets
in the Growing Gills Workbook at http://jessicaabel.com/gg-reader.**

Materials: Put your hands on that piece of paper on which you wrote down your one goal for the next 6 to 12 weeks, and how you will know when you've achieved that goal, and get out your QTAs worksheet from the Workbook.

Step 1. In order to break this big baby down further, you need to dig into the component parts. One of the most productive ways to do this is by writing down all the questions that occur to you about it. This list of Questions To Answer (QTAs), a concept I picked up from Nicky Hajal*, will help you later create action steps that make sense. Keep the list with you whenever you're thinking about your project (i.e., probably all the time) and add QTAs whenever you think of them.

Example case:

Your goal: to make your first podcast episode.

Start with the end result, what you know already: **It will be a podcast episode.**

Possible Questions to Answer (QTAs):

- What do I have to have done to call it finished? Is it only making the podcast, or also uploading to iTunes, or at least Soundcloud?
- Then: What are the steps that go into making a podcast?
  - › How should I write it?
  - › What's the overall theme and purpose?
  - › What's the style?
  - › How will I produce it?

Step 2. Break down each of the steps.

Example case (continued):

- What's the podcast about?
- What's the podcast called?
- Am I interviewing anyone? Who?
- Do I need a script?
- What's in the script?
- Should I have a co-host?
- Do I need training to edit?

---

* *http://actionally.com/library/a-simple-way-to-make-progress*

- Can I find a collaborator who can edit?
- Where can I find reliable mic reviews?
- What's my equipment budget?
- Do I need to prepare a space as a studio?
- What's involved in soundproofing?
- How can I figure out which editing platform is right for me?
- Who's going to make my logo?
- How do you upload to SoundCloud?
- Where is my password for SoundCloud?
- Can I connect SoundCloud to my blog somehow?

...And so on.

Step 3. Break your list of questions down further. Each individual question you've identified may house a whole slew of sub-questions.

Example case (continued):

Take question 4 from the preceding step's podcast example: "Do I need a script?"

Sub-questions might include:

- Is this a fully scripted show, or is it recorded live?
- What kind of intro and outro do I need?
- Is there someone who can edit the script with me?

Step 4. You may also be asking yourself some meta-project questions. Note these down, too.

Example meta-project questions:

- How can I create a system for developing upcoming ideas so that I've always got a pipeline?
- How do I carve out time from my schedule on a regular basis?
- How do I retain excitement in my project? *stay motivated to big picture*
- Do I have to write every day to be a real writer?
- How can I stop planning and start working?
- How can I create a consistent practice?
- How can I find others to work with in real life?

• How should I structure my days to be most effective?

Some tips to keep your anxiety in check:

- If you're the type to keep writing more and more questions, driving yourself crazy with how much you don't know, stick to the following rules of thumb:
  - › Keep your questions as concrete as possible.
  - › Set a timer: Do this activity for 30 minutes only.
- Phrase the questions in open, positive ways that encourage answers rather than defaulting to self-judgment (e.g., "How can I figure out the tool I need for X?" will prove more useful to you than "Why am I such a lazy idiot?").
- Don't subdivide the list and make it neat. We'll do that later.

Step 5. Once you have your QTAs list started, take a step back and think about how you might categorize your questions. Don't make shiny new lists yet; just think about the various ways you might—later—group things in a helpful way. Make a few notes on the worksheet or in your notebook. Some general examples of categories for QTAs follow below, but these categories should be aligned to whatever fits your individual project.

Example categories for QTAs:

- Idea pipeline
- Schedule
- Drafting
- Mindset
- Promoting and marketing
- Technical production
- Existential questions
- Training
- Research
- Team
- Networking
- Financial

Step 6. Hold on to the QTAs worksheet and carry it around, so it's handy when you have a brainstorm.

Time-bound tasks:
Quotas

When you're dealing with open-ended creative work, like creating a draft, you may not have any idea of what kind of timeline is realistic, **especially** if you're relatively new to this kind of work.

This is just how drafting works. You're going to be tempted to make what appear to be "action steps" like "draft Chapter 3." But, really, that's not an action. That's a project, with multiple steps inside of it. Here's what an actual action plan for the project "draft Chapter 3" might look like:　　　　　 *learn to point*

- Review outline of Chapter 3.
- Mind-map* Chapter 3.
- Write 500 words a day on Chapter 3. (Or, alternately: Write for one hour a day on Chapter 3.)

This last bulleted item in the above action plan, the quota task, might be a step you repeat twice, five times, or even 20 times—however long it takes to complete the chapter. That depends on how long, complicated, or difficult Chapter 3 is, and you may not know that while you're working on it. But I guarantee that if you work on Chapter 3 every week for a set number of quota sessions, you **will** finish drafting Chapter 3.

---

* *A mind map is a visual way to think through and break down the elements that feed into an idea. You start with a central idea, then create branches for components that feed into that idea, then sub-branches for elements that go into those components.*

1. question
2. action
3. add to system

QTAs to actions:
Start at the end

Your QTAs will come in handy at this point. You can turn all those questions around into actions, and then put the actions in your system.

For example: If you're wondering how to break down production and delegate some of it, first ask yourself, "What's the first thing I need to do to figure this out?" You can't break down production without knowing what's *in* production, so you mentally walk through production of whatever the project is and list what needs to happen.

If your project goal is a book, you need to concretely imagine all the questions and steps involved, working backward from the future final product, which might look like this: "OK, I have my book in my hands. How did it get here? It was shipped. By whom? The printer. Which printer? I need to find a printer. Who knows printers? My pal Greg has published books. I'll ask him. How did the printer print my book? I had to give them files. What files? What format?" ...and so on.

When you work all the way backward to the question "How did I create a final draft of my book?" you've reached the beginning of "production." At that point, you can take all those actions you just imagined, put them into a logical sequence, and *then* you can identify which parts of the production process you need to do yourself, and which you can delegate.

Some of your QTAs will likely be research-based: "What software? Drafting methods? Ideal work process?" Your thinking process here, as you map these tasks out, should center around asking, "Where can I go (or who can I ask) to figure this stuff out?" Make a list that includes those research resources.

Activity:
Breaking down a project into actions,
Part 2: The forest and the trees

**Find this activity and any relevant worksheets
in the Growing Gills Workbook at http://jessicaabel.com/gg-reader.**

Materials: You'll need your One Goal and your QTAs so we can break them down to produce next actions. You'll also need your "trusted system" at hand: a digital task-manager or paper planner.

Step 1. Project stages to actions: A good way to start breaking down projects is to identify the basic **stages.** You'll have started to think about these in the context of QTAs.

Although some projects will require different stages, for most projects, the stages probably look something like this:

1. Prep work
2. Drafting
3. Editing
4. Polish and presentation
5. Launch
6. And if you're a pro, marketing and selling

Each of those stages has multiple action steps.

Don't worry, you don't have to break them all down into those action steps right now. **In fact, don't.** All you'll do is get overwhelmed.

Step 2. Create headers for the various project stages. What you should do now: Create headers like the ones above for each phase of your project, so that as you have those random thoughts in the middle of the night, you have a preset place to capture them until you're ready to consider them

Step 3. Create action steps within the first project phase. Start with just the first project phase, because if you keep going, you may get overwhelmed, or you may fall down the list-making procrastination rabbit-hole and never come back.

Starting at the beginning, with the first task you need to do before you can complete any other parts of the project, use your QTAs to generate your list of actions. Put them in order. What is your next possible action? And after that?

Creating action steps within that phase means mapping out the following concrete details:

Measurable tasks. Pin down concrete things that need to happen, actual, finite tasks like "Read Wikipedia about giant redwoods, and take notes." These are tasks you can do in a specific period of time, finish, and check off.

Time-bound tasks (quotas). For more open-ended activities that are not as concrete, schedule chunks of time to lend structure to them. (Like: "Spend one hour working on mind map for my new blog series.") Because you've made that activity time-bound, you're more likely to do it. You can put it on your calendar, do it for the allotted amount of time, and then check it off your list. If you're not done in one hour, you can schedule a second session. But making the task time-bound also allows you to stop and move on to new things after that hour is up. You won't feel trapped by the task or fall into self-blame for not finishing. This is what I call a Quota task.

Step 4. Make sure your action is defined as an action. Use a verb. "Research X," "draft Y," "draw Z."

Step 5. How will you know when this stage is complete? If it's not obvious, write a description of what "complete" looks like.

Step 6. Some of your QTAs just won't have steps yet. Brainstorm a bit, but don't force it. Sleep on it and see what comes. When you leave an open-ended item like this on your list, though, identify it as a **project**, not an action.

WARNING: The work in this chapter, where you ask questions about how you'll achieve your goal, and then break the project stages down to actions, is likely to make you want to freeze up because you're looking at the whole enormity of what you have set out to do. You have to do this from time to time, to plan out strategy.

But as soon as we get this big-picture structure in place, the goal is to get back to that 5-feet-ahead focus. Don't look at the whole project. Look only at what you need to do NEXT. That's the beauty and the power of next actions. The irony is you need a bit of the scary 10,000-foot view to get there.

Chapter 10

Your Ideal Week, Next Week
Creating a responsive and effective schedule
based around your real daily life

In this chapter, you're going to take what you've figured out about your most effective conditions for success, your task list of open loops, and your famous time-tracking calendar, and you're going to create a picture of an ideal week.

But not just *any* ideal week: You're going to make a calendar for *next* week, taking into consideration your priorities, your actual life, and your actual tasks, in combination with your creative projects.

What you choose to spend your time on right now may be whatever is most Pressing. But you can choose to commit to other priorities. ***Your calendar is the physical manifestation of your priorities.***

However, in order to create that calendar, you need to identify and calculate two things:

- First, you have to know what your priorities actually are.
- Second, you need to know exactly how much negotiable time you have— that is, time with enough flexibility regarding how you spend it to be able to make a choice about your activities.

Once you've assessed both criteria, work toward lining those two factors up.

Working with your particular reality

The idea here is not just to write down whatever you happen to be doing. It's to challenge and stretch yourself to think more thoughtfully about allocating your time, without losing sight of who you actually are as a creator, how you work best, and what you need to do already in your daily life.

This is meant to be your ideal week, based on how you would like to be working *in your present-day reality*. In other words, for the purposes of this exercise, you don't get to imagine how great it would be to not have a day job if you have one. Whatever is currently nonnegotiable on your real calendar stays nonnegotiable. There's no point in imagining that you have three hours to write when, in reality, you only have 20 minutes.

You also don't get to imagine that you're a person who can power through six-hour creative sessions, if that is not who you are. You may be able to bend that curve over time, but you may not ignore who you are as a person and as an artist when thinking about how you want to be spending your time *next week*.

The discomfort of this exercise may give you a weird, third-person objective look at yourself. That is exactly the point. If you see your own activity in that more distanced, dispassionate way, you will begin to recognize and make use of your own agency, taking more active control over your decisions with a mindset of conscious intent. That impartial perspective is key, because when we let our more familiar, subjective, first-person selves rule this roost, self-judgment kicks in pretty quickly, and soon enough we're again being tossed to and fro by the vagaries of our Pressing open loops and letting those shifty winds push us back into unconscious, passive default decision making.

My most important, core revelation in doing this work on building creativity into our real lives is that we rule over our own decisions, both the ones we make consciously *and the ones we don't*.

That's the good news because it means we have the agency to make different choices if we want different outcomes.

The bad news is that we have to *use* that agency, to make conscious, intentional decisions, no matter how tough the dilemma we face. | A

The options we have available to choose from during some periods of our lives can be really hard to grapple with—during challenging times, the spectrum may feel like it goes from crappy to apocalyptic—but in my experience, whether it's about your art or anything else that's important in life, it's very rare for there to be only one choice, one way, one decision, one path, and it's even rarer for the default, passive action to be the best of the possible options.

What does all that mean for your calendar? It means that even when mapping out your ideal week, you only have the hours you have. So the issue is having a realistic idea of how long it takes you to write, not necessarily (immediately) writing faster or more efficiently.

What I can guarantee you: You'll find that even defining what time you actually do have available, even if it's an incredibly small amount, will ease up your anxiety. If you literally have 20 minutes next week to do creative work, what's the point of beating yourself up over it?

What happens over holidays for just about everyone is very instructive in underscoring that last point. During holiday times, we just blindly assume that our creative lives should carry on as they usually do. But most of us have many more commitments and interruptions than usual. Even if we don't, and we aren't technically busier, whether it's because of who and what we do have in our lives or who and what we're missing or both, holidays tend to be a highly charged, draining time of year for everybody. Both life's joys and its sorrows are heightened.

The point is that irrespective of your personal situation and temperament—irrespective of whether holidays are your favorite times of year or they are tough, depressing periods you just need to "get through" as quickly and uneventfully as possible—holidays take up more energy, so you're likely to be more depleted than usual even if you have free/negotiable time. The best thing to do is to acknowledge that, and give yourself full permission to do the things that you need and want to do that are NOT creative work.

Whatever happens during your holidays, holidays only require two action steps for creative people of all backgrounds: 1) Forgive yourself. 2) And then make a calendar for the next week.

I can hear the skeptics out there grumbling after reading that last paragraph: "*Even if she's right about the holidays—and I'm not saying she's persuaded me fully on that—how does that help me with my calendar and my creative work during the rest of the year?*" Here's why I said that what happens at holiday time can be instructive in more general terms: In order to get better at all the skills that will enable your creative work (e.g., aligning your priorities with your negotiable time, consciously making decisions, defining your time, using all that to map out your ideal week on a calendar that you can use and try out next week, and so on), you also need to be willing and able to employ those same two holiday "steps" as needed—to learn to rely on them when you're struggling, to let them help you power through whatever obstacles you're encountering—throughout the rest of the non-holiday year.

⚑ Forgive yourself. And then make a calendar for next week.

Your time is valuable

Setting up a schedule ahead of time is about *valuing* yourself and your time, and choosing to use the time you have according to *your* priorities, not someone else's. When you see that you actually *can't* take such-and-such a project or task on, or it'll throw your priorities for the week into chaos, it becomes a lot easier to say no.

Or if you realize a new task actually is a top priority for you for such-and-such good reasons, you move other projects and tasks aside and make the time. But you do so thoughtfully, understanding the impact this will have on your other work.

Monotasking

When you're planning your week, you're going to face some hard choices, and you're likely to think at some point or another that you can just multitask, and get a couple of things done at the same time. If those concurrent tasks are cooking and listening to a podcast, OK, I'll let that slide. Anything more taxing, however, forget about it. You can't talk on the phone and write email. You can't write your essay and watch a movie.

Why not?

First, you only have the minutes you have. If you're reading email for five minutes, those are five minutes you're not writing your novel. But it gets worse (and this point is especially important for creative people): It can take many minutes, or even hours, to get fully tucked into a cognitively demanding task like writing (or answering email, for that matter). Each time you switch tasks, you may lose five minutes or even an hour of full effectiveness. This is called "context-switching."

And those lost, context-switching minutes are dangerous. As you're context-switching and not yet fully engaged in the next activity, you are highly susceptible to distractions. That's when you end up on Facebook without knowing quite how you got there. Even if you don't, the quality of the work you're doing across all the activities you're multitasking goes down: Chances are high that you're doing a lesser job of completing all those tasks in any meaningful way. Getting lesser results means either having to live with those shortfalls or having to go back and spend more time cleaning up your shoddier work. (And you guessed it—both those things tend to use up whatever time you thought you were "saving.")

Given all that, is it any wonder that a Hewlett-Packard study carried out by the Institute of Psychiatry found that multitasking causes the equivalent of a 10-point drop in IQ?

So what's the answer? Monotasking. Create blocks of time devoted to one thing, and let yourself get deeper. Even admin blocks devoted to phone calls and email will be more efficient and effective if not interrupted by your Vital creative work.

Priorities and choosing to face your dilemmas

In the activity below, I will ask you to go through all the things you're hoping to get to next week and *decide*, with conscious intent, which are your highest priorities.

When I say it this way, this might sound like an obvious thing to do. But we never do it. I wasn't able to do it until very recently. I knew what I wanted to focus on in general, but to identify, concretely, in the time available *this week*, what was most important? Either it 1) hadn't occurred to me to do that, or 2) I hadn't yet recognized the value of doing that and/or 3) I hadn't developed the skills needed to actually do it.

Making these choices ahead of time is incredibly valuable. It allows you to weigh your choices thoughtfully and not just scramble from one thing to the next as you try to hit all the items on your to-do list. It forces you to face what choices you are already making in this way.

Is your creative work truly *Vital*? You're here. Clearly you've decided that it is. But that's not the choice you've been making with your time up until now, week after week. What have you been choosing instead? Consciously or not.

Those answers are painful to face. It's painful for me sometimes to admit where I have chosen to devote my time. What I'm *actually doing* is what I have been making my highest priority. Again, consciously or not. And when that does not line up with what I think I want, well, it's no fun to have to own that.

But without owning it, without facing that head on, you can't make the changes you want and need to make. And again, by "owning it," I don't mean punishing yourself for it; I mean taking responsibility for it, first by recognizing it as a choice, and then by realizing that that means you have the power and agency to choose differently if and when your choices aren't working for you for whatever reason— today, tomorrow, next week.

Here's the key to why this is so hard: Every choice you make, even a very positive one that gets you where you want to go, carries trade-offs.

We talked about this in Chapter 1. You will have to give things up: If you choose to spend three hours next week on your draft, those are three hours you will not spend on something else. Watching TV, browsing the internet, playing video games: Those are often easy pleasures about which to say "it's worth it" to give them up. (And, unfortunately, they are also so dopamine-producing and attractive that it's very hard to *actually* give them up.)

OK, so what if the trade-off isn't just "guilty pleasures" but three hours spent playing with your toddler, making dinner, or doing housework?

What if the cost is actual money? Say three hours of paid work?

What if the cost is purely psychological? You know your Should Monster will just have a field day when you first get back to writing.

What will the trade-off be?

Identify all those trade-offs. You can use the Five Whys activity in Chapter 1 to help. WRITE THEM DOWN. And decide—TODAY— specifically what you are willing to give up or demote or delay for the sake of your creative work.

This is how you reinforce your decisions ("I knew this was coming. I knew this would be tough.") and take the process of sticking to your guns a little bit out of the realm of pure willpower.

Here's another tip: Identify and write down what it would cost you to *not* do your highest priority. What will that feel like? Who else will it affect? What will it gum up or prevent from happening? What will it do to future-you's life?

Activity:
Your Ideal Week

**Find this activity and any relevant worksheets
in the Growing Gills Workbook at http://jessicaabel.com/gg-reader.**

Materials:

- Your trusted system (task manager) with your open loops and your One Goal QTAs and tasks in it.
- Your time-tracking calendar, which, if you've been doing it even a little, will give you a picture of how you're actually spending your time.
- Print out another blank week calendar, or print out *next week* from iCal or Google Calendar, or whatever your go-to is. Use the *week* view, not the month view.
- Some colored highlighters or pens, as well as a pencil.

Step 1. Set up your pre-existing conditions.

- Mark out all the times you know you're already committed. Use one color for all the various things that happen every day just to keep your world spinning: sleep, get kids out the door, work, shower, cook dinner, eat.
- This is important: Use a different color to mark out times to relax and be with people, your friends and family, or to do leisure activities like watching TV or playing games. Those time commitments reflect your values, and whatever your choices are in that arena, if they align with what you want out of your life, treat them as non-negotiables. Then, when you're doing those things, don't waste that time worrying about what you're not doing (i.e., your creative projects).
- Mark activities like your commute with a different color, because that's one of the few times you may be able to use more efficiently by

multitasking (e.g., by listening to a podcast, if you're driving, or doing reading/research or even writing if you're on public transport and not packed in like a sardine).

- Schedule *blocks* of time for admin tasks: email, bills, phone calls, open loops. If you don't schedule specific time for it, this kind of work will end up eating up every minute of your available time and make you feel like crap to boot. Give it a home and then respect those boundaries.
- Now, make like my mathematician student Rebeka, and literally add up whatever remaining open time is left. This is where the rubber hits the road. Give yourself a number for the week. That will start to give you an overall sense of whether what you're telling yourself you plan to accomplish in a week is even possible. Once you can see what time is potentially available, and you see what you're actually doing, you can start to make mindful decisions about how to spend your time. Even if you find you've only got 15 minutes a day that's uncommitted, that's a start. You can get real work done on projects if you actually use that time well.

Step 2. Give your highest priorities space on your calendar.

- Take your task list of everything you want to be doing next week. Pressing, Vital, all of it. If you tried to write this all into your calendar, would it fit? I mean, literally, could you even get it all on there? I'm betting not.
- Therefore, the next step is setting priorities. Mark the items on your list that are your highest priorities. I know this is hard, but it's a lot easier if you're looking at the whole list and not facing having to choose what to actually do, right now, in the moment. It's a little more abstract. If you're using a digital task manager, you might create a "project" called "Focus" or "My Priorities" or "Hot Stuff" and drag your top three or four high-priority items in there. Or you might use tagging or flagging for this.
- Give your highest priorities slots on your calendar. Guess as closely as you can how long they will actually take. (You'll get better at this estimate with practice). You might consider also what time of day to schedule certain activities (something you can refine once you've

discovered your best times for work by doing the Creative Marathon in the next section). Use a pencil. You'll see why in a minute.

- When you run out of room (*when*, not if), look at the next highest priority still on your list. Is it higher priority than something on the calendar? If so, put it into the calendar, and take the other, lower-priority item off. Maybe it's not as important as a thing on Tuesday, but more important than a thing on Thursday. Maybe then that Thursday thing is more important than something on Friday.

- You **may not** put more items on your calendar than you have hours in the day. And if it's not on your calendar, it's not on your list for the day. In your task manager, take off any due dates that are not reflected in your calendar. Don't let items go red on you when you have not actually made time for them. That's your Should Monster talking.

- Move things around until your actual time in the calendar represents your highest priorities. Next week, as you try to do what's on your calendar, it's natural that certain tasks will take longer than you thought, and other things you hadn't planned for or scheduled time for will come up. When that happens and it's something you decide is high-priority enough for you to take on that week, that's OK; however, you need to adjust the calendar accordingly, by saying , "OK, I've got to bump something. What's the lowest-priority thing in my scheduled week that I can postpone and move to do later?"

- You **may not** schedule every available minute for work. That's just setting yourself up for failure. Procrastination will happen, work emergencies will happen, sick kids will happen, life will happen. **Scheduling yourself so that reality feels like you've screwed up is not allowed.** Leave blank "flex time" or simply call certain blocks "work or whatever" so you know it's OK to change plans.

- Always remember: The calendar is the concrete representation of how you spend your time. If your calendar doesn't reflect your highest priorities, you simply *will not get to them*. Put them on the calendar.

- Finally, ask yourself: "What are the trade-offs I'll face by making these choices?" Write down what you're willing to give up.

Step 3. Next week, put this calendared, ideal-week plan into action as best you can, using it as a guide each day, and then track and evaluate your actual time spent on top of it, considering these questions:

- What did you intend to do, and then what did you actually do?
- If there's a differential between your intended actions and what you really did (and there almost always is), spend some time contemplating why. Does that shortfall reflect an unrealistic expectation of what you can finish? For example, if you scheduled the task "finish Chapter 2" but your actual work was 30 minutes of writing, none of it useable, consider what might account for that gap. Was it just a rough or slow day creatively, which is OK and happens sometimes for no reason we can identify? Or was your estimate of how quickly you write unrealistic? Or does it come down to concrete choices you made that you can make differently next time?

Step 4. Plan the next week, taking into account what happened during the previous one(s).

- Spend some time considering what you learned during the previous week(s), both what worked well and what time was spent less effectively.
- Use repetition of the above technique to gradually bring your actual time use and your ideal week into better alignment each week, by changing behavior and also by recalibrating your own expectations.

Tips for the Ideal Week activity

Once you identify your highest priorities and the best times of day to work on them, a best practice is to schedule those slots out several weeks in advance, and then treat those times like doctors' appointments. You can change them, but it's a huge pain in the ass, and rescheduling really inconveniences you and the doctors. Sticking to your guns often lies in the realm of learning to say no to people who want your time during those slots.

Some people like to assign themes to days—Monday is for layout, Tuesday is for blogging, Wednesday is for meetings. That can be a helpful way to choose where to focus on a given day.

Some of your non-negotiables will be slightly negotiable, in that you may find better ways to group them so that you have longer productive stretches. You might decide to get to bed earlier so you can use the morning, or make sure your poker night starts at 8 p.m. and not at 6 p.m.

When things go off the rails, don't abandon the calendar. At your next available minute, stop, think, and REPLAN your day. Do this as many times as necessary! Your goal is not to rigidly stick to your calendar at all costs; it's to be thoughtful about where you're devoting your time and energy and adjust accordingly as needed.

If scheduling every last minute of your day makes you feel like the air is being choked out of your lungs, try grouping things together so you can mark out larger blocks of time and have flexibility in the way you go about doing those things. For example, call an hour "admin" and don't fuss about how that breaks down between email and phone calls. Just make sure you know what your priorities are for that block of time.

If you've got tiny children at home, your day will not be fully predictable. But usually nap times and the like even out to some average amount over the fullness of the week. Naps are not generally a high-concentration time, though, so perhaps assign admin or other less demanding work to those slots.

You're looking for your sweet spot: regular practice, not over-committing to the point where it's damaging your health. Remember: Creative practice equals self-care, but so does exercise, eating properly, and sleeping. Take care of your body so it can take care of you.

In general: Schedule your hardest-thinking, most creative work first, and leave admin, relaxing, and chores for when you're likely to be low-energy. I know this is obvious, but it takes real willpower and discipline to plunge into the hard stuff first thing, so putting it on your schedule and deciding ahead of time that this is what you're doing will help shore you up when you're feeling weak.

If you've got the problem of too much unstructured time, and you don't know what works for you, try setting up a couple of different structures for your day, test them, and see which works best.

This is an "ideal" calendar because it's what **could** work. It will not be reality. Please, please, forgive yourself when it doesn't work (notice I didn't say "if") and just get back up and keep moving. If you fall off the wagon, welcome to the club. There is not one among us who has not. (In fact, I've got a little secret for you: *There is no wagon.*) Getting this right takes practice! You won't hit 100% the first time out. Maybe not even the first year out. Aim for better, not perfect.

I recommend repeating this exercise for at least the next three weeks. I do this every week myself.

Your calendar will take time to start to make real sense! That's completely understandable. We all make wildly unreliable, usually overly optimistic predictions of how long things take until we really pay attention (and sometimes still even then).

This is the key lesson:

Your job is to focus on **what you actually do** in the real world, as well as on **what you want to achieve,** and then slot the steps toward those priorities into realistic time frames. Blaming yourself and letting the Should Monster take over is worse than useless: It slows down your progress.

And you're not doomed to whatever your current work efficiency is right now forever! Both factors, negative self-talk and your ability to get things done, can move over time. But you are working with what you have on hand right now. Doing that consistently is HOW you shift those factors.

Part 3: Aligning your Today with your Tomorrow

Growing Gills • Jessica Abel

What we're doing in this section

In Part 1, you defined what (used to) stop you. In Part 2, you built an incredible powered exoskeleton of a system that will help you achieve your creative (and life) goals.

Now it's time to build a large storage locker for that machine and never look at it again. Right?

Riiiiiight.

The tricky thing when it comes to systems is not building them, it's actually using them. That's what we tackle in Part 3.

What you'll achieve in Part 3:

- You'll identify how you've worked best in the past, how you can apply that knowledge moving forward, and how to build flexibility and understanding of your multiple life roles into your creative system.
- You'll implement creative routine into your life.
- And you'll build in a robust review process that will consistently realign your daily activity with the lodestar of your larger creative and life goals.

With these pieces built into your process, you'll build trust with yourself and design a creative life that will sustain you indefinitely into the future.

142

Chapter 11

There Is No Finish Line

How to look at your creative practice as a part of your overall life rhythms in a sustainable way over the long term

W e've talked a lot about prioritization in terms of "which project when." However, underlying the practical question of what idea or project to focus on creatively is the *much bigger question* of how to weave creative work into all the other things you do and want to do. In other words, how to build a sustainable system for your *life*.

You're here because you've decided that making self-generated work is essential to your well-being. I'm all for that. Now, what else is essential?

How about family? Friends? Those relationships are, in some senses, the easy essentials to acknowledge. What about carving out time for other parts of yourself, whether that's making time to exercise, see art, join a book discussion group, take walks, engage in political activism, travel, or, you know, sleep?

Living as a creative person is a lifelong marathon, not a sprint—and not to be macabre, but unless you reach some point when you decide that your creative projects are less of a priority, it's a marathon with no finish line until you die. That's both the good and the bad news.

In running, trying to train for and run a marathon as though it's a sprint leads to injuries as well as to burnout and unfinished races. Endurance running requires steady pacing, not concentrated bursts of speed. Likewise, when we treat every creative project as a sprint, it's exhausting, it's not conducive to our best work, and it even puts us in danger of hurting our physical and mental health. Creative "cramming" may work for a short period—maybe you can jam through a month writing some huge amount of time/number of words every day without acknowledging your true creative rhythms—but how will that play out over the long term?

In contemplating both what you want and what is sustainable for you over the long term, consider the following kinds of questions:

- Do you want to create a whole graphic novel *series*?
- Do you want to be on top of the podcasting game, not just this year, but in 30 years?
- Do you want to be painting, or singing, or writing poetry at 90?

I also often hear people talking about grasping their creative dreams in terms of their mortality—not knowing how much time they actually have left in this life—and wanting to be doing what's really important before that inevitable end.

That mortality filter *can* help us figure out what really matters. But if you're an average, middle-class person in a developed country, it's more likely that you've got many years left, and jumping into your creative work with the passion (and the frenzied anxiety) of the scared-straight is not really the long-term answer for most of us, even for those of us who have actually had that near-death experience.

What may be more relevant and motivating is thinking in terms of integrating creative work into your life so that it's a healthy, reliable, and even joyful part of what you do. Ultimately, you need to consider that hitting your creative stride takes sustained long-term practice at your craft, so if this work is important to you, you'd be wise to start that lifetime marathon training sooner rather than later.

To make that a sustainable proposition, you need to find and hone creative practices that work along with the other parts of your life and self. For me, the ongoing question is: How can I weave my creative work into my day-to-day life in such a way that I'm fully engaged with it, so that I neither get scattered and lose focus nor focus so intensely that I give up all the other priorities in my life?

[handwritten margin notes: dilemmas — solitude — manage tv + internet con... temptation — manage novelty needs of adhd]

Creative practice as self-care

In short, this book is about discovering and accepting who you are, externalizing and acknowledging how valuable your creative practice is to you and to your well-being, and exploring how you will integrate this creative work into the rest of your real life.

You're here because you care about your creative work, and perhaps you are sometimes able to do it, but you feel out of control of this process to the extent that it feels miserable. And this is true even for those of us who are working creative professionals. Even when we are actually *functionally* working, we've got those internal, nagging voices, saying, "I should be better at this."

Working with the creative person you are—today

Finding that elusive balance between your various selves and aspects of your life requires working with who you really are, creatively and otherwise, not the person you wish you were or who you might someday be in the long-term future. You can build a creative practice that's reliable, one that will support you as you make your creative work week after week, for as long as you live.

But that will mean first taking a hard, honest look at who you really are as a creative person. It will mean that you may very well have to stop pretending to be the kind of person who:

- sits down every day for six hours and just cranks stuff out
- does the work without any external motivation or validation *[handwritten: would love recognition + connection]*
- gets up at 5 a.m. and works for two hours before the kids are up
- gets up at 5 a.m., works until noon, has a three-course meal, plays nine holes of golf, and then naps
- works through the night, every night, cranking out page after page, hundreds of pages a year
- effortlessly builds a following, is constantly wired into the world, but is still able to do the work *[handwritten: watching tv]*

- doesn't have to work for a living and so can devote infinite amounts of time to creative dream projects
- embodies whatever and whoever it is that you're *not* but that you're telling yourself that you *are*.

Discover how you work best

We spend a lot of time reading and thinking about how *other* people work—specifically how they seemingly work better than we do. Those stories may be real or mythical (and they are certainly annoying) but, regardless, we compare ourselves to others, and that is absolutely no help. The way other people work simply can't be a model for our own work while we live in denial of who we are creatively, and of the other people and demands in our own lives.

Case in point: I had a conversation a couple of years ago with my husband. Matt is a brilliant artist, always diving deep into some new formal experiment. He does workshops and expositions, gallery shows and posters, you name it. But he beats himself up, thinking that he's got to speed up the pace on his books, because he's had this idea that "real" cartoonists have a massive body of published books out there. "Real cartoonists" put something out every year or two. And Matt wasn't reaching that standard.

After 18 years together, I finally realized, and said to him, "You know what, Matt? You are not that guy. That is not how your creativity works. When you're boxed into cranking out one project—even if you love the project—you're miserable. You have to change it up often. You don't want to be at your drawing table working only on one thing for eight hours a day."

Matt's still got that vision hanging over him of having 20 books under his belt by now. It taunts him. But gradually he's coming around.

And the fact is, he *doesn't* have 20 books under his belt. That is *water under the bridge*. Focusing on that phantom pile of books is not just a distraction; it's an excuse to *not* do the things that need doing to make *this* book happen. What he does have is a lively curiosity about and a body of research on new approaches to creating stories, and an international network of readers, fans, and co-conspirators. He publishes in translation journals and poetry anthologies, curates exhibitions and runs workshops. He makes music. And he makes books. Just not as many as he might like to be making.

I have a different rhythm, and some envy it. I have very little trouble with procrastination, and I can easily work eight to 10 hours solid, even on the same project. But my problem is that I can't get myself to stop. I have a workaholic tendency; that's what I struggle with. I tell myself that I enjoy exercise, but I spend eight to 10 hours at a time glued to a screen. I tell myself I'm a reader, but I've barely cracked a book in years because I've taken on so much, and I feel stressed and busy all the time. I get creative stuff done, yes. But I don't let myself breathe. It's not great. *[handwritten: I need external pressure + deadlines / rely on]*

I've got a friend who reports that she can work in intense, concentrated bursts of energy, but the day after that burst ends, she's toast. If she tries to keep it up (and she usually tries), it's worse than counterproductive. It brings on self-blame. Why can't she tap into that energy today, too? What's wrong with her?

We all have work to do on understanding how we work best, and where our weaknesses lie.

But here's the plain truth: Feeling guilt and anxiety is an optimum creative state for exactly no one, and that's what you get when you expect yourself to show up to work one morning with a personality transplant.

The first step, obviously, is that you have to value the work. It's your right and responsibility to use your creativity. Stake your claim. You're doing that.

But then treating the work as if it's something that should just *happen* because it matters to you is a recipe for failure. We're real people with real lives, and we don't magically know either how to make time or how to structure our lives so we can do the work.

Your job is to clearly see and accept who you are right now. And then if you have creative goals that you're not meeting (and who doesn't?), to gradually align your imagined life and your actual life more closely by changing your behavior, but **also by adjusting your understanding of who you are and your corresponding expectations.**

[handwritten: tiny steps / method to / building up / creative / practice]

How do I best work?

Activity:
The Creative Marathon

**Find this activity and any relevant worksheets
in the Growing Gills Workbook at http://jessicaabel.com/gg-reader.**

Step 1. Look back into the past, and think about a time when you worked at your best, when you were reasonably content, you felt the flow of creative energy, and you made good work. (And if that feels like too high a bar, think back to a moment when you were making something and you realized that your creative work was a non-negotiable, no matter how painful the process might be.)

What were the conditions?

Questions to consider:

- What was the nature of your creative project?
- Were you working alone or collaboratively?
- Did you have external or internal deadlines?
- Did you receive internal or external rewards?
- What time of day were you working?
- How many hours at a stretch? In a day?
- Was it very regular work, or in bursts, or just the occasional session?
- One project, or many projects at the same time?
- What kind of feedback were you getting? From whom?
- What was your environment like?
- What else can you remember?

Step 2. Compare that to other times when you've been in the groove. What details from the list seem to be commonalities?

Step 3. What could you do to replicate the conditions that seem to aid your success?

External motivation
and validation

Central to the feeling that this battle for your creative life is so deep, and so scary, is the common but mistaken belief that you have to fight it, and win it, alone. After all, I just said you have to stake your claim, right? Doesn't that mean you have to struggle through all your doubt and resistance yourself, solo, without some kind of external motivation (deadlines) or validation (approval) for your work? The answer is no.

You're getting a lot of tools in this book that you can implement alone. You're learning how to use them, and how to choose which are for you, and which are not. But that may feel…inadequate.

To keep going, you may feel the need for someone to tell you you're on the right track, that you're doing a good job. You may need someone to care about the result.

This desire for outside validation is rooted in the fact that creative work is self-generated and self-motivated, and you may lack confidence in the validity of your ideas, so you feel like you need permission.

In our individualistic society, which says that "believing in yourself" is both a sign of strength and an innate trait rather than a learned skill, wanting outside encouragement may feel "weak." That dynamic is one of our biggest shame triggers—because it feels like a sign that you're not cut out for this, and that you're not the independent free spirit you wish you were.

But you can't *talk* yourself into self-belief. To own that confidence and feel it authentically, you have to repeatedly *act* in a way that builds up your trust in your own creative impulses over time. In other words, you have to make your work.

The process of doing the work builds confidence, but you need confidence to do the work.

Catch-22.

Before you get all tied up in knots over this, let me remind you that we're a social species. We're programmed at a genetic level to maintain and build social bonds, to care what people think. In addition, creative work is at its root about communication of ideas and thoughts and feelings from your brain to others. That's a collaborative act. So can we just put this one to rest?

It's OK to need external motivation and validation.

It's normal. It's just *highly inconvenient at times.* You've got to build systems around making sure you get enough of it to keep going. Even simply realizing that this is what you need, and then saying, "and that's OK, the important thing is the work," changes everything.

Sometimes, those systems you build for external motivation and validation will need to be creative.

For example, I have a student named Brian who set out to create a graphic novel, ideally before his first baby (already on the way) arrived. He saw the need early for accountability, and he used my podcast group to move his project forward, getting feedback from fellow listeners. But when it came to actually biting the bullet and getting the script completely done, he was dithering. He posted bits and pieces but couldn't make himself draft the dialogue.

I was completely utilitarian in my advice: I told Brian, "Go find some external motivation until such time as you don't need it and it becomes automatic."

Here's what Brian did: He pre-paid an editor to read his manuscript, one who would charge extra if he was late turning in the draft. (Spoiler alert: He got it in on time.)

Obviously, the ideal is to be able to rely on intrinsic motivation. That would be awesome. But when you're way out of whack with your creative practice, that might just not be possible (yet). For all of you who can get to work if you have deadlines and paychecks from others, but always skip your personal work? I've got bad news: I have not invented a magical "intrinsic motivation implant." You will have to work up to it.

Building intrinsic motivation is like building a muscle, like working out. At first, it hurts like hell, and you need a workout partner or a personal trainer to hover over you counting reps. Eventually, the pleasures of the workout itself outweigh your resistance. AND once you have the habit, it just becomes what you do. (Anyway, I've read that that's what happens when one works out regularly...I wouldn't know, ha ha...)

The journey to being more internally motivated starts with accepting and working with the fact that you're **externally** motivated. If you can build a consistent practice, it will begin to be self-reinforcing. After a while, it will *create* internal motivation, which you'll reinforce by checking it off the list, feeling a sense of accomplishment. But if external motivation is what will build the habit, start by ensuring you've got that.

So. If you need external, extrinsic motivation, like a deadline, or outside approval, don't waste time beating yourself up over it. FIND SOME.

Some more ideas for creating external motivation:

- Set up a coffee date with someone to review your work (and theirs). Whoever doesn't get their work done before the session pays.
- Form a writing group.
- Form an accountability group (see below), a group designed specifically to help members stay motivated and on track, as opposed to a critique or writing group, which is focused on the quality of the work.
- Set up a date with a friend to talk about your work, with a promise that you'll provide work to review X days in advance.
- If you have tiny children, up the external motivation ante by setting up these commitments with someone else, then hiring a sitter, possibly paying in advance, or arranging free childcare with someone. The aim is to heighten the stakes enough that it would be a crying shame not to use that childcare wisely.
- Can you have a Skype or in-person meeting with someone you admire? A former prof, a colleague?
- Does none of this motivate you enough? What about putting cash on the line? http://www.stickk.com, https://www.beeminder.com

What all these ideas have in common is that **something is at stake**: your reputation (with someone whose opinion you value), your money, your free time. Figure out what you value enough to motivate you to not lose any of it, and you have your path to developing an effective external motivator.

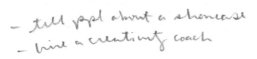

Get yourself some external motivation:
Accountability groups

An accountability group is a group of three to 10 people who are responsible for encouraging and giving feedback and support to one another on getting creative work done. This is not the same as a writer's or critique group, where you will share the work itself and get feedback (and if you're not getting the work done, you simply don't get feedback). It's a group whose focus is the question: How can we help each other do creative work more effectively and painlessly? For this reason, you can easily form heterogeneous groups of people in various fields who all struggle with the same basic problem of giving time and priority to self-generated creative work.

Who do you know who's also making creative work, who you might ask to become part of an accountability group? Identify three to 10 people you can ask, with the goal of forming a group of about four to six.

Note: If your answer is "no one," first of all, is that true? Think about your school friends, your Facebook friends. If you can't think of anyone, it may be because you wouldn't dare ask the people you can think of. Maybe consider whether that's reasonable, or an irrational fear.

If you can't think of enough people, join a local writer's or other creative group, or join a creative group on Facebook, and put out the call there.

What are the stakes? Name what will happen if you fail to show up and participate in your accountability group. Make sure the stakes are high enough that you can use them for motivation.

What are the benefits of forming relationships around your work? Name some of the good things that could come from regularly showing up and supporting others, and getting support, around your work.

Activity:
Setting up an accountability group

Find this activity and any relevant worksheets
in the Growing Gills Workbook at http://jessicaabel.com/gg-reader.

Step 1. Aim to put together a group of no more than three to 10 people.

Step 2. Either invite specific people to your group, or post a call in a social media group you belong to.

Step 3. Set up your criteria for members clearly:

- Is this group for accountability and encouragement? Concrete feedback on work? Operational support? Collaboration?
- What medium, or does it matter?
- You might also consider physical location/time zone.
- Pick a preferred platform—Facebook, email, or live interaction, in person or via Skype or Google hangouts? (An occasional face-to-face could be a good idea even if you normally do this via written formats.)

Step 4. With your group members, schedule meetings at a set time or day every week and establish a format. At the most basic level, it can be this simple:

- Report whether you've hit your goals for the week. You can also talk about why things went well/didn't go well.
- Set new goals for next week.
- Request advice, feedback, and suggestions for improvement. One note: If you or someone in your group is consistently setting high goals and missing the mark, make sure you address whether the goals need to be adjusted.

Pressing vs. Vital

It's common for us to get caught up in a swirl of doing Pressing tasks, to the exclusion of Vital work.

To review this idea: Pressing tasks are loud and obnoxious; they demand attention. They are promises and commitments you've made to yourself and to others (sometimes not even realizing that's what you're doing) that feel like *you've got no choice* but to do them right now. This is why you're able to get work done when you're paid and contracted, or when you've got a deadline in a class. Someone's waiting for this. It's PRESSING.

Vital work is the work that builds your creative practice and your body of work. (Alternatively, it could be work that is deeply meaningful to you in another way, such as volunteering, caring for a sick relative, spending unstructured time with your kids, or taking care of your health). It's easy to skip Vital work, because it does not *demand* attention. But when you skip it, you start to feel like a total jerk.

You may not feel entitled to take time for yourself in this way. It might feel selfish, but it is the opposite: You need to put the oxygen mask on yourself first, and then you can be the person for others that you want to be.

You may have lots of Pressing work to do, stuff you really can't skip. That's OK. One of the alumni of my Creative Focus Workshop commented on this idea as follows: "Structurally there are systemic things that are putting more and more and more pressure on people (especially women who are caregivers and income-earners). *Self-protection and self-care are important precursors to creative productivity.* And productivity (measured by product) is maybe overrated?"

She's absolutely right. If this chapter is giving you hives rather than helping, you're putting too much pressure on yourself. **Creativity is self-care, but self-care is also self-care.** If you're not sleeping, not eating properly, making yourself sick, that comes first.

Use what time you have
with intent and without guilt

Once you understand that self-care can and should come first, you will find you have small segments of time during which you have room to do the Vital stuff. You're likely doing it already, but in a state of panic, beating yourself up the whole time.

When your time for Vital work is limited, instead of berating yourself or trying to fight or deny that reality, simply admit: "I've only got 15 minutes for this. Not a lot will get done. That's OK, but I'm going to actually *use* that time." And then you have to do it, even if it feels like a ridiculously short time. Do it.

Taking action on a regular basis will move the needle on the work, whether it's as fast as you'd like or not. You may not have the option to concentrate on your book for a four-hour stretch. But you can find 15 or 30 minutes, and you have to make sure you treasure those minutes like the gift that they are.

Chapter 12
The Big Creative Rhythms
Being a Parent, Being a Partner, Being a Child

We're all familiar with the idea that we each have times of day when we work at our best. Some of us work better early in the morning, some at night, some right after lunch. What we talk about less often is the fact that we have periods of our *lives* when we work better, and periods when it's more challenging. Just as it's wise not to fight your natural circadian patterns too hard, it's also a good idea to recognize that there are times in your life when other things than your work will take precedence, and that's OK. That's as it should be. *or a pandemic where it's longer on to leave your house*

When you have a newborn baby, or your parents or spouse are ill and need constant attention, you're not going to be 100% present for your creative work. If you can recognize that, and also see that the time period in question has an end point, then you can forgive yourself for not getting your butt in the chair every day, and do what needs to be done. Remember, it's a marathon, not a sprint.

On a less intense level, if you're a person with relationships that matter to you (and I sincerely hope you are), the time investment—and sometimes work—needed to maintain those relationships and build them is one of the most important jobs you have. Building that time into your plan for your days is part of what you need to do in sorting out and categorizing the Pressing open loops in your life.

All that said, again, even if you feel like you've got an unmanageable amount of commitments to your household, figuring out how to inject some balance into that by carving a bit of time out for your personal creative priorities is more than justified, it's crucial—even if it's minutes at a time, and not hours.

Balancing creative practice
with specific phases of parenthood

As a parent myself (and fortunately not having yet had a sick parent or spouse to care for), I've had some thoughts about how to go about balancing your creative practice with parenting. First of all, it changes over time. There are a number of distinct phases, and remember: No matter what people say, for the vast majority of us, life is long.

1. Newborn shock and awe.

When you have a newborn, your ability to focus on almost anything else is rightfully out the window. To me, this calls for forgiveness, not more "shoulds." Take a sabbatical. Sketch, read, and make notes if and when you can; the first three months are tough on sleep, but babies at that age also don't do much, so you'll have some non-focused but useful time. Then start rebuilding your practice around the new reality.

2. Munchkin land.

If you have kids who are younger than school age, you have an enormous amount of daily labor to get through, above and beyond whatever you had to do before the kids came—much more so if you're staying home with them and don't have child care. This change does two things: First, you get much more efficient about your time. It may not feel like it, but the fact that you can be wiping butts 15 times a day and also doing *anything* else is actually super-impressive. You've probably blown past your previous productivity records without even noticing it. Second, on the other hand, your daytime-hour concentration is shattered because you could be on call at any moment. Brigid Schulte calls this "time confetti"*: Your

---

* http://www.smh.com.au/lifestyle/health-and-wellbeing/wellbeing/brigid-schulte-why-time-is-a-feminist-issue-20150309-13zimc

individual free minutes might add up to hours over the course of the week, but they're pretty useless when you're in that contaminated state.

When you're in this phase, it's easy to get depressed about your limited ability to concentrate on your work. This is where looking at your personal creative rhythms, planning your week, and *getting as much help as you can* is really important. But you also simply have to acknowledge: This is a full-time job. But you are doing something enormous, important, and fulfilling, and if you get less creative work done in these years, that's OK.

3. School years.

This is where you start to get your brain back...gradually.

Your free time and concentration get better as the kids get more self-sufficient and self-entertaining.

I know tons of creative people who basically fell off the map for 10 years, especially those first five, but then the productivity and skills they learned from parenting, and the deep desire to do the work, saw them roaring back as their kids matured. Cartoonist Dylan Horrocks, for example, came out with several important books in the late '90s and early aughts, then virtually disappeared from the scene as raised his kids for 10 or so years, and recently has been just about everywhere with a few new prize-winning books.

Forgiveness, not self-blame, is crucial. Just do the best you can to fit in the time. By adding more complicated humans to your household, you've permanently altered the amount of undisturbed time you can devote to work, at least until they move out (and probably even then). That's OK. You've learned so much about what's important to you and how to manage your time. This knowledge will help calm your nerves and help you identify how you want to work and when it's possible. You may not hit ideal, but you'll move forward.

4. Teen spirit.

Teens are a whole new phase, and one I can't (yet) speak to from experience. Other parents tell me that this period really will give you more control over your time and attention, but teens are also needy in a whole new way. It sort of sounds like you'll gain a relationship with an extremely touchy and demanding but interesting friend—one who calls on you to be 100% present at random and sometimes inopportune times, but who can also leave you be for long stretches. My student Louise says, "I found it helpful to build in some regular time alone with my son (now 19 and at college), like pizza together or a short road trip—that way stuff that would otherwise have surfaced when *he* needed it to would have been dealt with already. Sometimes."

Balancing creative practice
with parenthood in general

In all phases of the parent-child relationship, the process of thinking through what is actually happening in your life already, and how you can make conscious choices to modify your use of time and attention, will help calm your nerves and identify how you want to work and when it's possible.

There's a common fantasy out there that being a writer or creative of any sort requires total control over time and freedom from constraint. We imagine that one's got to have a life like Jack Kerouac or William Faulkner or Sigmund Freud—in short, male, self-centered, destructive, and catered to or enabled by mostly invisible women—to create.

This is the dominant understanding of what it means to be an artist we hear from everyone from Cyril Connolly, the 20th-century critic and writer, who famously said, "There is no more sombre enemy of good art than the pram in the hall," to Virginia Woolf in *A Room of One's Own*, which is both a feminist cry for equal access to time and space and a reactionary embrace of the idea that the only way to be fully creative is to reject domesticity and live more like a man.

Kids are wonderful, *and* they take up part of our lives. Even admitting that you *want* to focus on your own work can be guilt-inducing when you have kids. What is "enough" when it comes to spending time with them? By way of an answer, one of my students whose kids are on the verge of adulthood (and needed mostly not to be smothered) had some very good advice: "Commit to your creative practice publicly in front of your child and bracket off whatever time-space is feasible for now. Because when they are older, one gift you can give them is to be passionately absorbed in something that is not them."

Everyone in the family should have the right to follow their interests, including you. If that means one less kids' class or playdate or party, that's something they should come to understand. Mom gets mom time, and Dad gets dad time. That's a healthy thing for kids to learn to deal with. Not easy to manage, of course, but healthy.

Kids also don't have to derail you (all the time). Having to balance their needs can give you greater focus. I've personally gotten much more fiercely productive and creative since having kids. Before having kids, I was never able to just get up in the morning, have a cup of tea, and get to work. Now, I do that daily. That "get up in the morning" part includes getting two little ones up and out the door, but once they're taken care of, I value my work time intensely. I just sit down and start.

Ultimately, as parents and creative people, as long as we look at what makes up our real lives and don't dwell on how others do things, we'll be OK.

Chapter 13
The Value of Routine
Embracing creative routines as the source of inspiration and joy in the work

We are suspicious of things that feel too easy. One of the things we train kids to do as they grow up is to stick with it through struggle. And that *is* a very valuable skill, don't get me wrong. But when we rely *solely* on willpower to make a project happen, we're setting ourselves up for failure. Willpower is a vanishingly scarce resource, and we have to use it for all kinds of things, all day. As we use it, it is depleted. Why waste your willpower when you can create routines that avoid forcing you to face decisions that will be hard to make?

Sit'cher ass down

We've all heard the advice about solving creative productivity problems— which mostly boil down to sit'cher ass down and get to work. Everyone knows that the answer to "I don't feel like writing" is "write anyway." But we still don't do it. Why?

Waiting for the muse:
Inspiration is a bill of goods

You can envision the work you want to make today, right there in front of you. It's just there...on the other side of this bottomless pit of anxiety.

The temptation is to wait for "conditions to be right" to sit down and get to work. That's totally understandable: When you're trying to create, but you don't really know what you're going to do that day, you'll sit there worrying about what you're doing and whether it will be any good. You have tons of ideas, lots to say, but when you sit down to work you might feel that:

- *I don't know all the answers.*
- *I don't know how to say this.*
- *What will people think?*
- *My desk is a mess, and I've got to start dinner in 15 minutes.*
- *I'm not inspired.*

Those doubts are what feels like a trap, like this dark pit between you and actually making a project happen. And who needs to fall into a dark pit? You start scrolling through your email or your Facebook feed.

You know from experience that if you can just get *past* that pit, you'll be in the creative flow, and you won't worry about any of that stuff. You'll actually *be* inspired, and it will feel amazing.

Naturally, you want to get over there, to that feeling. But facing the very present emotional danger on the way is not an attractive prospect. And it takes enormous willpower to force yourself to do it when you feel unconnected to your work.

My friend Donna was tied in knots in exactly this way over some articles she needed to write. And the worst part was, she felt like she was the crazy one. She was sure that "other people" don't get stuck:

> *There are probably other sorts of people out in the world where this isn't a problem that just makes them go, 'What the fuck?' And stop. There are other people who don't come to a screeching halt here. But I do.*

But I believe most of us are like Donna. I believe that the vast majority of people *do* come to a screeching halt. Sure, some people don't, and we look at them and say, "Why can't I be like that?" A lot of people think I'm one of those people.

But I'm not. I've spent many a good hour not-writing blog posts, not-writing my next comic, not-writing this book. I know all about the not-writing. When I reassured Donna that she's normal, that I get stuck too, she went on:

> *I actually thought there was something totally wrong with me, and that I can't actually do it, because it takes so much time. It feels like I'm thrashing.*

> *And then I do produce something and other people say that it's good. But I'm aware of all the shit that went on behind the scenes, and it's exhausting to think about starting that over every week.*

Exhausting is exactly the right word for it. By forcing yourself to *decide* over and over—to quit whatever you're doing now, to sit down, to not do the hundred other things you might be doing, to focus on your work, to not look at your phone when it buzzes—you exhaust your reserves of willpower, and very quickly you'll have none until you replenish it by eating or sleeping or both, and so you'll start making (non-)decisions that you'll regret.

That's no way to write a book (or make a painting or whatever).

The key to sitting your ass down to work isn't willpower. And it definitely isn't inspiration. It's systems, and it's *habit*.

The painter Chuck Close said:

> **"Inspiration is for amateurs.**
> **The rest of us just show up and get to work."**

Daily practice is not about feeling good about the work. It's not even about making something good. The practice *itself* is how you make space for great ideas to strike you. Not every idea is going to be great, every day. Many won't be. But you open up a space where you could have those ideas. If you're not working, there's no space for inspiration to arrive.

Great. So we're back to "sit'cher ass down and work." Thanks a lot, Chuck Close. So helpful.

I've heard that quote over and over, and it's a great one. But I looked it up, and what Close says next is actually much more interesting, and much more helpful:

You sign on to a process and see where it takes you. You don't have to invent the wheel every day. Today you'll do what you did yesterday and tomorrow you'll do what you did today. Eventually you'll get somewhere. Every great idea I ever had grew out of work itself. If you're going to wait around for the clouds to open up and lightning to strike you in the brain you're not going to make an awful lot of work.

Signing on to a process

This is the most important part of what Chuck Close advises: "You sign on to a process."

Yes, you need a regular creative practice. But there's more: How do you build that practice? By having a system for working, a specific way in which you go about doing things day in and day out, so you never have to start from scratch. You establish a routine.

If it's easier just to work than not to, because *that's just what you do at this time of day,* you'll do it more often.

That may feel "uninspiring." But in my own creative life I've found no truer words than when Chuck Close says, "every great idea I ever had grew out of the work itself." The words you write or the marks you make today soak into your unconscious, your mind plays with them while you're not paying attention, and when you come back tomorrow, you've made new connections. If you don't come back tomorrow, those connections start to fade. Not to say that every day produces genius, but the process is more than additive, it's compound. The richness of your relationship with the work grows exponentially as you return to it day after day.

I don't blame people for thinking that's not how it works. That's not how it works on TV or in movies. That's not how it works in books. Why? Because it's boring to watch an artist do the real work. No one makes art about making art that captures the process faithfully.

Think of a painting like *Las Meninas* by Velázquez. It's exquisite, immense, and exciting. There's so much to discover, the king and queen in a mirror's reflection, the maids and the court dwarves and the dog, and Velázquez himself. It's a scene you want to jump into, to inhabit. It makes painting look exciting.

Well, I've watched painters paint. It's engrossing and exciting for them, inside their heads. It is not a rip-roaring ride from the outside. So the process is rarely depicted, or if it is, it's depicted inaccurately, in romantic, idealized ways that often compress the true amount of time involved. (C.f. the entire "bohemian" mythology—epitomized by a show like *Rent*—that lionizes poverty, suffering, and hanging out as fonts of creativity.) This more exciting, fictionalized depiction of creative processes may account for our heroic idea of what it's like to be "struck" by inspiration.

Passion—and inspiration— come from investment

Let's take this a step further. What if you're not sure what you're working on is really what you are destined to do? How can you know for sure? What if you've picked the wrong thing and this is all wasted effort?

There are so many people depressed and anxious about not knowing what they were meant to do, as if there were really only one thing we were meant to do.

Passion for a practice or a subject comes from your investment of time and energy.

Whatever your passion, it is a combination of what you're into, and your circumstances, and what happens to fall across your path. It comes from what makes you feel great. That might be a personal sense of fulfillment, but it might just as well be how much you can help other people. Being a mother or father is the passion of some people. Just doing a good job and being a good colleague is the passion of others. If you don't have a passion for writing or art or whatever "high calling," just look for what you can do that's useful, that gives you pleasure, and do more of that.

I've always loved stories. But I started out totally crap as a storyteller. I had to work very hard at it, for many years, to be any good at all. And now, storytelling as a craft, as a set of tools, is a core element of my work and a central research concern of mine. **But that's not destiny. That's investment.**

There are times when you'll feel that fire for whatever it is you want to do, and you can't wait to jump out of bed in the morning and get started. And there are times when that thing is a job. There are times when you feel you will never ever want to do it again. But you get up and you do it anyway. You go to work. (Not "get to work," not "do the work," *GO* to work. Because it's your *job*.)

That's how something becomes deep and nuanced and important to you.

That's how you develop expertise and special skills that may be valuable to others, or make something the world hasn't seen before.

You have the power to choose what you want to do.

You do not need to feel trapped by whatever you think you "must" be doing creatively. Maybe you want to make music. That can play out in dozens of ways, and you need to be flexible and inventive about how you're going to actually make that happen in your life, especially if you're trying to make a living as a creative person. And that means: possibly finding things to be passionate about that aren't exactly what you thought you'd spend your time on.

Having a great idea & paying attention to your attention

One of the most common questions that authors get asked is "Where do you get your ideas?"

Because it makes it sound like art comes from a magic vending machine, it's consequently one of the most commonly mocked questions by authors, but it isn't a dumb question at all. Quite the contrary. The problem is not that it's dumb; it's that it makes some assumptions that professional artists and writers know to be deeply faulty—that ideas come from somewhere specific, fully formed, and they strike us with a touch of the ol' genius, and then off we go.

That's not how ideas work. Or rather, that's not how good ideas work. Sure, they start with some spark or notion, but that bit could be as flimsy as toilet paper ("cheerleader who fights vampires," anyone?).

What makes ideas great is what you invest into them, how you dive deep, find new angles and resonances, and build the ideas from the ground up.

So. You want to know where I get my ideas?

I pay attention to my attention. I follow my taste, and I dive deep, investing time and energy, until I have something worth sharing with the world.

A few years ago—actually, quite a few; it was in December 2006—I was working on my textbook about how to make comics, *Drawing Words & Writing Pictures*. I collaborated on it with Matt, and we were working on a chapter about how to create characters.

There's an activity in that there we'd done many times in our classes, where you randomly choose a physical characteristic, a job, and an emotional characteristic, and then you put them together, and you build a character out of it. It's funny, and fun, and it demonstrates definitively the power of juxtaposition—just put those non-aligned things together and your mind starts working. I can't tell you how many students have gotten bizarre combos like "melancholy jockey who wears colored contacts" and then gone on to actually love those characters and use them in stories.

Anyway, I had Matt give me keywords for two characters, so I could draw some illustrations for the activity in the book.

Here are the prompts Matt gave me:

- cheerful
- spiked collar
- X-games

- worry wart
- wears a skirt
- tour guide

...And I came up with a roller girl and a seven-legged Martian.

The second part of the assignment is to put the characters together into a scenario and build a story structure. So I gamely put Trish Trash, my rollergirl, on Mars, then invented a wacky caper plot involving a stolen suitcase, and then drew another illustration to suggest that storyline. It was just an example for our textbook. I wasn't trying to come up with anything deep.

But days later, I still felt myself drawn to the idea. On Christmas Day 2006, I jotted down a few notes.

Six months later, I had read up on leaf-harvester ants, bee colonies, and various theories about terraforming Mars, and I was halfway through Kim Stanley Robinson's Red Mars trilogy. I went to a bunch of derby bouts and talked to players.

And as bits stuck to it, my idea grew from a silly Nancy-Drew-on-Mars romp to a massive, world-spanning story, touching on climate change, class conflict, and coming of age.

Trish Trash: Rollergirl of Mars debuted in the U.S. in November 2016, almost exactly 10 years from its inception. But it all stems from three prompts:

- cheerful
- spiked collar
- X-games

And Trish isn't even really all that cheerful anymore.

I paid attention to my attention, and I dove in, way way in. Eight years and two planets in.

There's a story in my book *Out on the Wire* about this process. As far back as 2005, Alex Blumberg, then a producer at *This American Life*, now founder of Gimlet Media, became curious about how all his very non-rich radio producer pals were buying houses. How were they getting mortgages? What was going on in the housing market?

> *I became sort of obsessed with all these websites that were talking about it. I got totally obsessed with this one website called "Calculated Risk." Early on in 2005 it was a place where skeptics about the housing bubble gathered.*

Alex worried that reading sites like "Calculated Risk" meant that he was just succumbing to alarmist internet rhetoric. He kept trying to pitch stories on the topic to *This American Life*, but nothing seemed to gel. He consulted his old friend Adam Davidson, who was a business reporter:

> *...And he [Adam] would tell me like, the people I talk to say there's not really a problem as long as the models are right. But you know, the models could be wrong. Ha ha.*

There was something about the subject that Alex couldn't let go of. And then the summer of 2007 came along:

> *...The first big subprime lender collapsed, which was a company called New Century, I think. Then a bunch of them collapsed after that. And then, I remember Adam sending me this email saying, "maybe it's too late to do that subprime story." I was like, "I think it's still OK."*

The 2008 story Alex and Adam made to explain what had caused our economy to virtually collapse is called "The Giant Pool of Money," and it's among the most listened-to, talked-about, important hours *This American Life* has ever made. And that episode, along with the reaction to it, is what inspired Adam and Alex to found the show *Planet Money*.

What's important here is not the success that the story became. It is that the germ of the idea that eventually made *Planet Money* possible, this weird tingly feeling about mortgages, seemed like a total outlier when Alex started poking at it and developing it. And then it took four years to come to fruition! Great ideas take patience. More than that, they take trust. You have to trust your own taste, your own interest in the idea, and follow it all the way down the rabbit hole.

what is "taste driving me toward?" [handwritten note in margin]

As Ira Glass says, Your taste matters.

And chances are, if you're somebody who wants to make stories, the reason why you want to make them is because you love stories, and you probably do have interesting taste. That's what's getting you into the game.

And how do you know what your taste actually is? You have to listen to yourself, pay attention to what excites you (or pisses you off), what you talk about. And then invest in it: Invest your time and your attention.

Finding and building ideas is a job in and of itself. This part of the creative process can feel the most slacker-y, the most guilt-inducing, because it might take place while riding a bike, obsessively Googling, looking at art, staring out the window, or showering. Allowing yourself to invest in your ideas takes trust. But knowing that this is a legit part of the process will help.

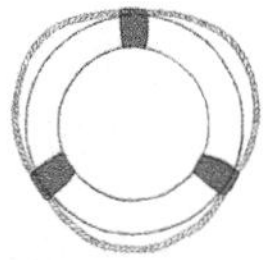

Getting started faster and more reliably

In order to get to work the way you want to, you need to address two main hurdles:

1. Activation energy and decision fatigue
2. Distractions

Setting the table

"Activation energy" is a term that comes from chemistry. It's defined as the minimum energy required to start a chemical reaction. Before that amount of energy is added to a system, nothing happens. As far as I can find, this term was first applied to human behavior by James Clear[*], who writes about changing habits. His theory is that you can create tiny new habits with a small amount of activation energy, and those tiny habits can build up over time; by contrast, creating a *giant* new habit will require a huge amount of energy all at once and up front, and thus will probably fail.

---

* *http://jamesclear.com/chemistry-habits*

Another way to talk about the same issue is *decision fatigue*, which is the result when you depend on your willpower to force yourself to take each next step in your project. Willpower being the scarce resource that it is, sooner rather than later you run out of willpower, and you're no longer able to force yourself to do the next thing.

You can see where I'm going with this. The goal is to reduce the amount of "activation energy" you need to implement to do the project you want to do, and in turn to reduce decision fatigue.

How?

James Clear continues his chemistry analogy by recommending *catalysts* in your environment that will trigger your new habitual behavior. Catalysts in chemistry are compounds that reduce the amount of activation energy needed to start a reaction. In your life, they will be small, easy activities that make doing the bigger stuff easier.

The specifics of those catalysts depend on what you're trying to do, but the basic model is: Avoid decision fatigue in the moment by literally setting the table for you to work. Take the tools of your trade, and get them set up for a work session the night before you plan to work. Remove all other options from view. Make doing the work the default option, and require an explicit *decision* not to work.

Examples of catalysts that set the table

If you're a writer, before you go to bed, quit your browser and email program, and anything else you commonly jump into first thing, and open your writing program to fullscreen or distraction-free mode. Then sleep the computer.

If you're a painter, get your materials out and arrayed for easy access right before bed. Set out your painting clothes for tomorrow. Even if you don't have the space to leave everything out all the time, you can certainly do so while you're sleeping, assuming you can arrange your life to get to work first thing, then clean up and start the rest of your day.

That's physically "setting the table."

To psychologically set the table to work, which you may also need, try Ernest Hemingway's ninja trick, as quoted in *With Hemingway: A Year in Key West and Cuba* by Arnold Samuelson:

The main thing is to know when to stop. Don't wait till you've written yourself out. <u>When you're still going good and you come to an interesting place and you know what's going to happen next, that's the time to stop.</u> Then leave it alone and don't think about it; let your subconscious mind do the work.

It's truly frustrating to work this way, to literally leave a thought half fin—

See what I mean? Frustrating! But stopping before "you've written yourself out" will absolutely get your subconscious engaged in working through the problem at hand. The same principle applies for any sort of creative work. Filmmakers can hold off on that next edit, cartoonists can stop inking mid-figure. It may mean you can't check off "finished X number of pages" in the same way, but if you have major getting-started issues, this "table-setting" for tomorrow's work will help. <u>You've intentionally created an open loop, and you'll be incredibly eager to get back to it just so you can finish up that thing you left hanging!</u>

Activity:
Set the table

Step 1: Tonight, clear and set your workspace as if you were about to get to work, set out work-appropriate clothes, and then go to bed.

Step 2: If you're just starting something, make a mark on it. Type these instructions into your writing software, or write a note on your page or canvas.

Step 3: In the morning when you get started, act before you think. Get started as if your creative work were as simple and habitual as brushing your teeth.

Step 4: Tomorrow, as you wrap up your work session, start to implement a thought or idea, but don't finish it.

Distractions

The other obvious offender when it comes to not-starting or stopping too soon is distractions. Whether for you that means games, social media or texting on your phone or computer, or tidying your house or watching TV, distractions are the easy fallbacks for filling your time. Your goal is to make them less easy, less present, when you want to make your creative work (or do anything else you're procrastinating over, for that matter). *Twitter, Netflix, Instagram, phone notifs*

Using your Time-Tracking and Creative Marathon worksheets, identify your main offenders when it comes to distractions. The key in those activities is to identify your most vulnerable points and implement countermeasures in those particular spots.

Be creative with your countermeasures! The idea is that distractions are normally the easiest thing to do in any given moment. If you increase the activation energy needed to fall into distractions, that will help keep you on track.

Examples of countermeasures for distractions: *"make it unattractive + inaccessible hard"*

Clean your workspace and other visible signs of open loops:

- Having cleaned your desk will be a help. Keep it clean. If your eyes fall on an open loop, that can pull you out of your work mode.

Most people have issues ignoring their phone. Pay attention to when and how it interrupts you, and implement measures to prevent that happening:

- Turn off the ringer and all sound notifications that do not reflect life-and-death needs (e.g., if you're a doctor on call).
- Turn off all lock-screen notifications.
- Or, turn off all notifications, period. If this makes you nervous about missing an email from your boss or a call from your kid, make them "VIPs" in email and "Favorites" in phone, then adjust settings accordingly.
- Delete apps that make you feel yucky when you use them but that you can't seem to stop using. (Many social apps and games fall in this category.)
- Move all apps off the first screen of your phone, so when you open it up, you see only your wallpaper.
- If your phone is too much temptation, period, remove it from view. Store it in another room, or in a purse or coat pocket.
- Set your phone to "do not disturb" or airplane mode at night, so nothing

comes in and pings at you. Refrain from turning it on in the morning until you do your Vital work. (Get an alarm clock.)

Explore possible countermeasures for other digital issues:

- Do you like to use Facebook to stay in touch, but often fall down the hole of newsfeed scrolling? Check out the Chrome extension News Feed Eradicator*.
- If other internet distractions are the problem, try https://selfcontrolapp.com or another externalized control mechanism for sites that are too tempting.
- Turn off wifi on your laptop, or turn off your router.
- If the computer in general is too distracting, use paper. Shut down your computer every day (not just sleep) and then work longhand or in a sketchbook in the morning before you allow yourself to turn it on at a certain time.

If you use cleaning itself as a distraction, narrow your scope and access to doing that:

- Make a clean spot to work in, and then turn your chair so you can't see anything else.
- Put a childproofing lock on the cabinet with your cleaning supplies. Yes, you can open it, but this deterrent is a reminder to keep your cleaning impulses in check.

Minimize excessive time spent playing video games and/or watching TV:

- Use when-then agreements to make gaming or TV a reward: When you finish X, then you can play or watch for Y time without guilt.
- Log out and shut everything down when you finish playing/watching.
- Put the TV in front of a really uncomfortable chair.
- Remove your console and remote controls from the room and put them in a closet when you're not using them.
- Loan your electronics to a trusted friend.

If attempts at countermeasures in your house or workspace fail, your countermeasure might involve changing your location temporarily:

- Extreme measures: If you have the opportunity, get a housesitting gig, or take a day or two in a hotel or AirBnB in your town or somewhere else.

---

* http://news-feed-eradicator.west.io

Possibly search for a listing with complaints about "bad wifi." Bring nothing but your work materials.

Activity:
Breaking down your own resistance

**Find this activity and any relevant worksheets
in the Growing Gills Workbook at http://jessicaabel.com/gg-reader.**

Just as you're tracking your time, your objective here is to track your resistance and distraction.

Step 1. Ask yourself the following questions.

When you attempt to focus on your creative work, what exactly are you doing when you feel resistance?

And what does that resistance feel like? The Should Monster? Fear? Or is it a lot less specific, something that simply feels like an unquenchable desire to play a video game or tidy the coffee table?

Does a phone or computer notification trigger it?

Does it come up right at the beginning of doing creative work, or after you start?

Do you simply just never get that far? Do you find a million things to do before you even face the work? What are those things?

Step 2. Write up a description of what is most likely to distract you and when.

Step 3. Once you identify when and how you're getting distracted, use the examples of countermeasures above to create a concrete, written plan to make it harder to fall into distractions.

Step 4. Implement your plan, test, and change your countermeasures where necessary.

Chapter 14
The Key is the Trust
Creating a robust review process that will keep your creative work on track long term

The most important function of systems that support your creative practice is to make it possible for you to work on a daily basis toward your goals, both creative goals and other life goals.

At the core, that's not just about making things to send out into the world, it's about being at peace with yourself. It's feeling a sense of security that you know what comes next. Every day, things are OK, you are on track, you're going in the right direction, and you can relax.

Your subconscious mind will reward you by not freaking out all the time. Because you're not freaking out all the time, your work becomes easier to produce. It's a virtuous cycle in which positivity reinforces good habits, which in turn reinforce and support the work you want to be producing.

Building a healthy creative practice is *self-care*. It's the best kind of self-care, the kind that builds you up from the inside. It may feel self-indulgent to spend time and money on your creative life when the rest of your life seems to be falling apart. But that's *exactly* why you need to do it.

If you think self-care means taking exercise classes, let's get this straight: You won't go to exercise classes if you're tied into knots over not-working. The core of self-care is taking care of the core of *you*. That's where the emotional turmoil you feel about your creative work lives. And that turmoil is what you will start to calm when you implement a reliable, trusted system.

So today we're going to add an *absolutely critical* layer to your system, one that will allow you to check in with yourself on a regular basis and make sure you're on track toward your goals.

I talk about having a "trusted system" in which you can place all your goals, track your progress, and plan your projects. But here's the thing:

The key is not the system, the key is the **trust.**

It may sound wild or paradoxical to say that, after all the time and space I've spent with advice on how, specifically, to create a system. That advice is real, and it's based on what I've found to be effective for myself and for peers and students who do creative work. That can all be helpful, to be sure, but the truth is, what an effective, trusted system looks like is highly subjective, and you can have whatever kind of idiosyncratic system you want to have.

You can invent a totally janky system, cobbled together only for you with bubblegum and duct tape. But if you can and do *trust* it to support your creative work, you've got what you need.

What Does "Trust" Mean?

Your subconscious is smarter than your conscious mind in a lot of ways. You know at some level that you're losing track of your goals when you're mindlessly going through actions and never taking a global look to make sure those actions really lead where you want to go. Or, for that matter, if you don't capture all your flitting to-dos in the first place, you know you're forgetting things. That's when anxiety kicks in.

"Great," you say. "I get it. But what does 'trust' in a system look like, concretely?*"*

You don't just pat your iPhone at night and say, "It's OK, I trust you." Trust is all about the system being there for you, to bolster you and support your weak spots, when things start to fall apart. The same way you know you have a friend you can trust because she's the one who takes care of your dog without being asked when an accident lands you in the hospital, that's how you know you have a trusted system. It's there when you need it most.

How the hell do you know your system is "trustworthy"?

When it comes to people in your life, you may know in your bones who you trust and who you don't and why. Often those determinations have been gradual and organic.

For your self-created system, however, you can and should be very calculated about building in features that will reassure your subconscious over time that *you've got this.*

What does that mean? It means building a robust **review** process into your routine, one in which you verify that you're moving in the right direction and take time to reflect on whether that is indeed the direction you want to be heading.

Trust in your system
stems from review

What does review mean?

It means you spend a bit of time regularly assessing where you are and what you've lined up for yourself and mapping those two things against your larger goals to see if you're getting closer. This sort of review should happen ideally on a weekly basis, but monthly can work on longer-time-horizon projects.

Here's what review might mean in practice in more granular, day-to-day terms:

- It means you look at your **next actions** every morning.
- It means you may choose to review where you're at in the evening.
- It means you literally read through your current projects in your system, ideally once a week, thinking about what might be missing and what you'd like to prioritize next.

switch to ytd, w/ tick tick? On OneNote?

Altitudes

The thing about your trusted system is that normally, on a daily basis, you should only look at it on a micro level. Focus only on the three to five things you want to get done in that day. If you look at the whole long-term future of your project all the time, it'll be like Kazu Kibuishi warns: It'll be like staring at the sun. You'll get paralyzed by perfectionism and will feel inadequate to the enormousness of what you want to achieve. Focus instead on the five feet of sidewalk right in front of you, and keep moving forward.

The limit to that approach is, you *do* need to have a larger strategic view of what you're aiming for, so you can realign yourself with that target. So you need to check in at that higher level every week to several weeks.

It's a question of shifting altitudes periodically to inform your overall perspective and process: You need to work daily at the 5-foot level. But you also need to understand the 5,000-foot view, and even, once in a while, take in the 20,000-foot view.

That need to shift altitudes relates to one of my major gripes with most planning tools: They do really well with atomizing your work into doable bits, but because they also obscure or outright ignore strategic view, you can lose yourself in pressing tasks pretty easily and never return to the big, strategic picture.

So you have to take it on yourself to pull back and really think about *why* you're doing what you do. You need to name your highest priorities, and make sure the work you're doing has you headed in the right direction.

That's what you're doing here, in this book, but it's also something you can commit to on a regular, recurring basis. I do a quick review every week, and a full version quarterly, when I plan my next 12-week goals.

Effective review depends on objective measures of success

When you're in the middle of a huge project, even if you review your progress regularly, it's easy to lose track of how and whether you're making enough progress week to week. Just thinking to yourself, "Did I do enough?" is a recipe for self-blame and getting derailed.

That's where creating objective measures of progress is really important. What are the actions that contribute, long term, to getting your Vital work done? Quota tasks like "write 500 words" and "sketch one hour," measurable tasks like, "lay out one page of the comic" and "meet my writing group," and also more meta actions like "do my weekly review"—they may not look like much individually, but added together, they are what a massive project is made of.

You will have actions like this on your list, but since they're so process-oriented and seemingly distant from your desired outcome, these are the easiest actions to skip and procrastinate on if they're not accorded proper importance and given time in your calendar.

Development and success markers

For your largest projects (usually the toughest nuts to crack), the key will be identifying development markers and success markers. Defining what's working along the way is one way to stay on track and ensure you build in work on your Vital projects on a daily basis instead of getting sucked into Pressing tasks from other parts of your life.

lag vs lead

Success markers = results

Success markers are **results**—the desired outcome that comes AFTER all the work. We all know what some success markers look like: It can mean a finished story or a podcast on the air, or it could also mean finding a publisher willing to produce your manuscript or selling X number of your creations. Success markers are what we dream about when we're imagining what will happen with this cool new idea—once that confusing and scary black box of *actually doing the thing* is somehow, mysteriously resolved.

But success markers do not always have to yield a new physical object, so long as there is an identifiable outcome. For example, more personal success markers might include spending a certain number of hours a week with your children or sleeping enough (which for me might be eight hours a night and for you might be nine; the point is that it's a specific, articulated outcome).

The key question is: What is your No. 1 priority? The secret to staying on track is revisiting that question periodically to check in with yourself and recalibrate your own expectations as needed—your No. 1 priority might not be what you think it is. It might not be just finishing your goal, but selling your creation so you're making a living. Or it might not be either of those results, but rather simply incorporating creative life and production into what you do in a non-anxiety-ridden way. We will talk more about this in Chapter 16: The Long View.

Once you identify that No. 1 priority, you can map out your most meaningful success markers. **If you're consistently hitting your success markers, that's a sign**

that you've been working in the right direction. Naming and counting success markers is important in acknowledging your achievement and celebrating it, and also in making sure you're headed the right direction.

Of course, as a careful reader, you will have noticed the big problem embedded in that previous paragraph. By the time you are totting up your success markers, whatever it is you're trying to make happen either has happened, or it hasn't. It's too late to change anything about how you're working to make sure you achieve "success."

Development markers = processes

Development markers are the small actions you perform on a daily and weekly basis that move you along the track toward those desired concrete results (or success markers). Without hitting your goals for your development markers on a regular basis for a long time, there will be very few successes to mark. That's why, as important as it is to quantify your success markers, it's even more important to identify your *development* markers.

The actions I named above, in the introduction to this section, are all development markers: quota tasks like "write 500 words" and "sketch one hour," measurable tasks like "lay out one page of the comic" and "meet my writing group," and also more meta actions like "do my weekly review."

Other examples might include actions like "spend one hour on my project with no social media," "take a walk to brainstorm," or even "take one hour of unscheduled time to dream." You undertake these kinds of actions regularly, and it may feel like nothing is happening, yet these actions add up to work being done.

If you're not sure what your development markers are, you might start by looking at the Creative Marathon activity. Are there any regular actions you took in your peak-performance times that stand out as key to your success?

Activity:
Using development markers
to chart progress and tweak processes

Step 1: Make a list of what you think your specific development markers might be. You may have a lot of candidates. Pick two or three that look like they will be the most effective processes in moving the needle on your work.

Step 2: Add the development markers to your calendar, and regularly perform those actions without thinking about what results (success markers) you expect, and you'll find correlations with actual creative work coming out the other end of the machine.

This is basically the definition of "trusting the system."

Step 3: You may also want to identify specific success markers, especially if they are not obvious to the naked eye, and track these on a quarterly basis. This is a way to test your hypothesis about which development markers are most important for your creative success. (**This is how you train yourself to trust the system: Trust and Verify.**)

Test and change

You may not know what your best development markers are. That's where semi-scientific testing comes in.

Set a specific development marker and test the process, by doing it for a certain amount of time, say, four weeks, or even the full six weeks of your project milestone. Check yourself at the end of that period by looking at your success markers. Did your development-marker actions produce results? Yes? Continue. No? Try a different marker.

For a really large project, like my book *Trish Trash*, for example, I initially use development markers that are quota tasks to mark progress: "Work 2-3 hours a day, first thing, on my script." Once there are actual comics pages to draft, my system morphs, and my development markers become more specific: "Lay out X number of pages today." "Ink X pages."

I find the development markers helpful because stages like scripting can end up taking a lot longer than I'd like, so if I don't chip away at it over a long timetable, it simply doesn't happen.

The distinction between these marker types is why you procrastinate less on administrative work than on so much of your important, creative work. It's so satisfying to cross stuff off a list! You feel productive! Having identified and scheduled your development markers as regular, repeated activities is how you get to cross "noodling" or "daydreaming"—or whatever Vital activity feeds your work, but doesn't feel like work—off a list, too.

This can be a scary way to approach work. Allowing yourself to do things that are potentially pleasant and that don't necessarily have metrics that let you prove to yourself that you're "working" can bring the Should Monster out screaming. One former student commented: "I feel like I'm doing a trust fall, and the 'friends' behind me are 'development markers.'" She's right. Once you've done the work to figure out that this is what you need, your job is to believe it.

After she took the Creative Focus Workshop, my student Amy Lewis has found herself coming back to these markers over and over, to her own surprise.

I have been creating word count for a week and it feels like nothing is happening in the story. So I'm coming up to the end of the six weeks, and I'm gonna summarize all of these scenes and I'm going to call it done. And I'm going to move on to the next thing. And I'm going to trust the freaking process. I hate trusting the freaking process.

I don't trust the freaking process. But I have to pretend like I trust it and maybe eventually I will trust it.

The thing is, it always bears out. I'm like "Ugh, stupid process! I don't even trust—!" And then sure enough, it actually works, but I never learn and it hates me. It's the worst sitcom ever. Like me and the process living in an apartment together like Felix and Oscar.

How do you make these reviews happen?

Reviews are literally projects and tasks in that self-same system you'll be reviewing with them. If you're digitally based, you set them up to recur and remind you, or if you're in an analog system, you place a reminder in your calendar to do these when they're due. Then, when the time pops up, you make a nice cup of warm, calming beverage, and you take 15 minutes (or longer, for big quarterly reviews) to take a look at where you're at, take things that you don't need to focus on soon off your plate, and put other things that are more immediate priorities on.

What you will specifically choose to review is up to you. Here's what I suggest, in general terms. Adapt these ideas to your needs. Keep in mind that some of these lists look kinda long. But the act of actually going through them really takes just a few minutes.

My Review System

First, I have a project in my task manager called "repeating checklists," and each of these lists is a subproject within that project. They are set to recur automatically at the right frequency. Again, if you're on paper, you can simply put your review time on your calendar.

My daily review components:

First thing every day, I have reminders for the following tasks:
- I check my calendar (and adjust if need be).
- I check my task manager inbox to move things I've thrown in there the day before into the projects they belong in.

My weekly review components:

Weekly, I do a quick pass of my various sources of open loops, try to consolidate everything into my trusted system, and check in with my larger goals:
- I go through my physical inbox to see if I'm forgetting anything.
- I clear off my computer desktop to dispose of distractions and open loops.

- I check my annual wall calendar. (This is where and how I check in with myself and envision longer stretches of time.)
- I review development markers and track them. (Literally, I count how many development actions I completed versus planned, and give myself a percentage completion rate. I have development markers set up on professional as well as personal projects.)
- I set up development marker tracking for next week.
- I read through my whole system, prioritizing and deleting items, spending a few minutes thinking about each project to check in with my goals.
- I file physical stuff that can be archived. (I often skip this one, honestly, but I keep it in my weekly review list to remind me that it needs doing to stay organized and to keep open loops from multiplying or growing. In practice, I aim for doing this filing once every month or two.)
- I do digital filing. (This is simply a digital version of my physical, analog filing. I have a digital "to-file folder," and again, as with the physical filing, I often skip it as a weekly task, doing this once a month or so.)

An alternate version of a weekly review

I'm including this second weekly review to underscore that different components work for different people. As you'll see, this weekly review includes a lot less tidying than mine does:

- Look back at your calendar for the week: Did your time go the way you expected? Did you have any moments during which you felt you were truly your creative self, and what contributed to that?
- Why did your time go that way, and what changes could you make to your calendar for next week that will give you more control over your time?
- What did you accomplish that advanced your highest priorities this week?
- What changes could you make to your calendar for next week to make more room for your highest priorities?
- Are you tracking ahead of or behind your development and success markers this week?

My quarterly review components

On a quarterly basis, I make sure to recalibrate my expectations and goals around my highest priorities:

- I check 12-week project progress against annual chief initiative and annual professional goals.
- I create new 12-week goals.
- I review on-hold projects, with an eye toward *deleting or minimizing Idea Debt.*
- For each project I'm working on, I'll also have a series of specific phases or elements I want to make sure I'm keeping an eye on, such as editing, production, and marketing.
- I review where I'm at on personal and family projects and goals, setting new benchmarks if need be.
- I look at my budget and revenue planning documents, track progress, and update with new info.

How much time reviewing takes

You've now seen my daily, weekly and quarterly review lists. It all sounds like a lot when you see all three lists spelled out in rapid succession. But actually doing it doesn't take very long at all, especially not once you get used to the routine of doing these tasks. My daily review takes maybe three minutes. My weekly review only takes about 15 to 20 minutes, a bit more on days when I actually do that filing, and, tellingly, they are **deeply satisfying minutes.**

How and when to schedule
your weekly reviews

As with most aspects of a trusted system, this one is all about what works for you and what routine is going to provide you with the greatest degree of support and the least amount of added anxiety.

I try to do my weekly review on Friday afternoon, so I can go home and really relax afterward, knowing I've got my ducks in a row. Even if I didn't hit my goals for the week, knowing where I'm at, and that the world won't fly to pieces over the weekend, makes all the difference to me.

Other people prefer to do this Sunday evening, or first thing on Monday, to get a fresh start on the week.

Whenever it is, once you figure out what works best for you, make it a ritual.

Accountability:
Others can help and remind you that
you're not alone

One of the best ways to reinforce your weekly review is to share it with someone else or a small group, as I discussed back in Chapter 11. Accountability groups have been the secret weapon of my most successful students from the Creative Focus Workshop.

How does it work? Each week, you do your weekly review, and in particular you count up how you did on your development markers. You then share your numbers with your group and reflect on what happened. How did you make your goal, and on the flip side, what stood in your way? Your group will celebrate your good weeks and help you understand your bad weeks, and together you can think through how to do better in the week ahead.

Review accountability groups and how to form them in Chapter 11 and in the workbook.

Activity:
Design and test-drive
a daily and weekly review

Find this activity and any relevant worksheets
in the Growing Gills Workbook at http://jessicaabel.com/gg-reader.

Step 1. Create a list of items for daily and weekly reviews.

- You can simply adopt mine if you like, but this list will evolve as you realize what you really need to be paying attention to and what works best for you.
- If the first list I've provided is too long and looks too difficult, try using the alternate version. But do read through your projects weekly.
- If, on the other hand, you'd like to try a (slightly more advanced) weekly

goal-tracking format that's been very successful for the students I've used it with, please see the six-week goal-tracking activity at the end of the next chapter, "Planning Backward."

Step 2. Schedule the reviews to happen at a set time every day and every week.

Step 3. Make sure you do your first full weekly review this Friday.

Chapter 15
Planning Backward
Developing a working plan for a creative project with a deadline

Picture this: You've got a hot idea for a screenplay. You know it's got legs. You daydream of being on set, of seeing which amazing actors will be standing in line to play a role, and most of all, of collaborating with the perfect director, whose vision is exactly aligned to make your words on the page into the film you've imagined and intended.

But you're not making progress on the draft. The whole project is threatening to turn into a giant pile of Idea Debt.

Then, your friend calls you and tells you he can get you into this very exclusive weekend retreat, with a small group, including your dream director. The dilemma: The retreat is in six weeks.

Oh, crap. *Time to get to work.*

Evoking this panic-inducing moment may seem to contradict everything we've done so far. I'm all about creating a system for chipping away on your big creative project that will get you to the finish line without anxiety, by focusing on the creative marathon: building creative work into your life in a sustainable way. Implementing that system may mean you will realize you've habitually set your sights too high in terms of output-per-year and will need to recalibrate your expectations. It's also likely to mean that you will actually *achieve* greater output per year than you have in the past (and will need to recalibrate your expectations).

But whatever your marathon-level expectations, you may still need to hit some specific external deadlines. Or you may even want to hit a self-imposed deadline because you need to move forward on a schedule for your own peace of mind and/ or life plan.

To hit a specific delivery date, you will need to create another layer to your system, one that ties your actions and completion to dates on the calendar. Other examples of deadlines, both self-imposed and external, that will necessitate planning backward from a completion/delivery date:

- You're scheduled to go to a convention at which you'll have a chance to pitch your book to editors.
- You're going to be a guest on a podcast whose audience is perfect for your planned course.
- You're invited to a party where it's likely you'll meet a successful blogger in your area.
- You're dying to quit your job by the end of the year, but you've got to get your website up so you can start making freelance income.

Sometimes, without an idea of the timeline and a concrete, identifiable deadline, breaking down a major project into a series of actions and getting to work is simply not workable.

So what do you do?

Find yourself a deadline and work back from there.

Identify (or invent) the deadline, and work backward

I recommend starting with a six-week goal. You can actually get your brain all the way around six weeks, so you're more likely to be realistic about what you set out to achieve. Even for me, while I do have annual goals, the more relevant, shorter-term timeframe for my goals is 12 weeks (or roughly three months). As I write this, it's January, and the first quarter of the great big yearlong calendar on my wall is packed full of activity and goals. The last quarter? Almost empty. I just can't really imagine what I'll need to be doing week-to-week in October or

November when it's still January.

So: Start with six weeks, and work your way up to 12.

Questions to ask to formulate a viable six-week plan:

- What do you want to finish in six weeks? (Envision the end.)
- What benchmarks do you need to have reached to achieve that goal? (Break down the phases.)
- What are the action steps that will lead to those benchmarks? (Break down the actions.)
- In what order do the action steps have to be done? (Put them in order, and put them on the calendar.)

This is really just an advanced version of what I walked through in Chapter 9. You have to break down your projects to individual actions before you can leave procrastination behind.

But the last bullet is an additional and essential step:

Once you have an idea of all the steps and subgoals involved in meeting your six-week goal, you need to put them on a calendar. Once you do that, it'll become immediately obvious that some weeks, you've scheduled undoable "actions" for the timeframe you've allotted yourself (i.e., those "actions" are secretly projects that you didn't realize were projects). In your calendar, these "secret project" items might read benignly (e.g., "finish Chapter 3"), or they could read as a lengthy, daunting list of eight or 10 subgoals you need to finish in one week—even if several of the subgoals will each take you more than one day, realistically.

In all instances, it's a matter of being honest with yourself about what's really possible in the time you've given for what you've outlined. The reason that's so important? Because plowing ahead with projects-that-you-think-are-actions is a recipe for failure and self-sabotage.

 If you see already that there is no way you're hitting the mark laid out in your calendar, *readjust your calendar or your expectations, now.* There's no point in making yourself miserable when you know what you are attempting is not achievable.

You've been breaking down projects into action steps, getting in touch with your rhythms, and imagining what an ideal week might look like. Now, we're going to look at slightly longer time horizons. This planning process is how you align your day-to-day creative activities with larger goals, and how you keep your eyes on the important, Vital goals as opposed to getting lost in urgent, Pressing day-to-day stuff. Though it requires some courage, planning like this is also how you avoid falling too much into Idea Debt Type P (for perfectionism), because on a daily basis, all you have to do is the three things on your list, not "write my novel." You may not feel ready to write your novel, but you can do three little tiny things, right? It's that micro-focus, guided by the overall plan, that moves mountains, one spoonful at a time.

By the way, I based this system on the book *The 12 Week Year*, by Brian P. Moran and Michael Lennington. The authors advocate 12 weeks as the longest period for which you should set concrete goals. And verifiably, your work (and you) can change so much in three months that it's (mostly) silly to imagine further out.

There are real reasons for imagining further out—this is how you choose the right path overall, the one that heads you toward the future you want for yourself. Knowing the right path is how you choose your projects in the first place. So we're still gonna imagine further out in the next chapter, the Long View, but for concrete planning, the six-to-12-week time-horizon is the way to go.

Once those initial six weeks are up, you'll need to set a new goal. Probably this will be the next phase of the larger, long-term goal you've already set and have been working toward. We're simply going to refine each phase and break down your actions week by week.

Then you'll get to work and *implement a weekly review to stay on track*.

An example of six-week goal tracking

The main creative goal over six weeks

In this example, the person's main creative goal is to finish a 16-page minicomic for an upcoming comics convention. That's a hard deadline and a concrete project. The artist has already done a gut check: This six-week goal aligns with her larger goal of publishing a graphic novel. With this mini, she'll make connections with colleagues and pitch a graphic novel to a publisher who'll be at the convention.

Identifying the six-week project's phases

First of all, she identifies the main phases she'll have to complete to get the minicomic done:

- Script
- Thumbnails
- Pencils
- Lettering
- Inks
- Scanning
- Cover
- Layout and production

Her development markers each week will be quota sessions on scripting and thumbnails, and page count when she's in production.

In a more open-ended plan that's geared toward developing a stronger creative practice, these might be purely quota-based development markers, such as:

- Write 30 minutes.
- Doodle 15 minutes.
- Take a walk.

Creating the six-week calendar

Then she breaks down the phases and her development markers over six weeks. She knows from painful experience that scanning and printing can take a whole week, so she starts there and works backward.

Her calendar might look like this:

Week 6: scanning and production
Week 5: inking, finish cover
Week 4: lettering, inking, cover
Week 3: penciling, lettering
Week 2: thumbnails, penciling
Week 1: script, thumbnails

She's got her work cut out for her. But it's doable, if this is the main focus of her time. She's got a part-time barista job, but that leaves her enough negotiable time that she can devote 30 hours a week to this.

Identifying goals in other areas over the same six-week period

Our hypothetical artist also has another goal: to improve her relationship with her mother. They've been fighting a lot, and she's feeling guilty about neglecting her. So that means investing a bit of time each week in that relationship, even as she works on her minicomic.

The point of including what may seem like an unnecessary or unfair curveball in this hypothetical scenario is that we all have (and more to the point, we *should* have) goals in multiple areas in our lives that run in parallel to the creative ones. You've only got so many hours in the week, but some of those hours you will want to devote to other things that are Vital to you, like relationships or your health. Set specific and measurable actions toward your goals in those areas, too, to move them forward at the same time as your creative ones.

Yes, this project is a sprint, not marathon material. Still, our cartoonist is a human being with many competing priorities, who has to face the dilemma of which to choose at any one time. So the goal here isn't to become a dedicated, hard-working artist for six weeks but neglect every other part of your life.

Think about it: That's unsustainable. You may manage to succeed in working only on a creative goal for six weeks to the exclusion of all other priorities in your life, and you may even finish that six-week creative goal. However, at that point, most people will then have to table or abandon the next phase of creative goals in Week 7 or 8 in order to shift gears and salvage the parts of life that they ignored for the previous six weeks, by giving those other life goals some serious attention.

Ultimately, the goal here is to acknowledge that no matter who you are, you'll have other goals you need to work on at the same time as your art, and that really your aim is trying to find some balance between those in *any* six-week plan you devise for yourself.

Assessing still more goals for the next six weeks

Our fictional cartoonist actually has six other goals as well. But she knows if she's going to get this mini made in time, she has to set those aside, and this comic has to be her **one** creative focus for these six weeks.

She has decided: This is the thing. She's doing THIS.

Speaking of which: Dilemma.

Finally, our cartoonist has tried to make some serious estimations of what trade-offs she will have to make to achieve these goals. She has written those down, and she has decided she's willing to take the hit.

Laying out the goals on a tracking sheet

Once our cartoonist works out the general arc of her project's progress, she can plug it into a tracking sheet and use it to look for trouble down the pike.

Doing that, she can see immediately that Week 3 is a red flag: "14 pages of pencils"? And that's assuming the script got done on time.

Week 4 is worse: "all the lettering, most of the inks"?

Those two red flags on the tracking sheet are the canaries in the coal mine for our cartoonist. If the minicomic is going to get done on this tight schedule, that's when she'll know.

Laying out the stages of work on a goal-tracking sheet is how you'll be able to predict your trouble spots **before** you get there. And if you know you're going to have a tough week, you can seek additional, short-term help **before** things get really dark. For example, you can ask your partner to take care of the cooking for a couple of weeks, warn friends that you'll be unavailable, figure out ways to cut yourself off from typical distractions (block your internet, lend your game console to a pal, delete social apps from your phone...), activate your support network, schedule focus sessions (see Chapter 17 for more on that idea), ask for editorial help, whatever you're going to need.

What happens if you're just not going to hit your deadline?

If you're working solely for yourself, toward your own future vision, and you're not meeting your benchmarks, your first instinctive reaction ought to be: "Hm. Maybe I didn't realize how long these things would take to complete. Let me adjust my expectations." And then you get right back on that horse, and keep going, *with an adjusted timeline.*

Avoid the temptation to browbeat yourself with shaming self-judgments, such as thinking, "I suck." You don't suck. Your timeline didn't work, and you can use that to inform a new timeline that does. Tomorrow is a new day, and next week is a new week.

If you have **external** deadlines that are nonnegotiable or that will have serious repercussions if you blow them, you may have to bump projects that are negotiable to give yourself more time to make the more critical, priority deadlines, or you may need to try to renegotiate the external deadline. For example, you might have to cancel that table reservation at the Comic-Con and instead show up with a new mini at the next time around.

But more generally, if you plan your work out ahead and give your plans a gimlet-eyed stare, you can probably figure out well in advance if your timeline is realistic or not. As soon as you know that, you can reach out to others concerned— collaborators, editors, readers, bosses, whoever—*and let them know*. No one likes to be told they're not getting whatever it is on time. But if they know well ahead, both you and they can make arrangements so that it doesn't derail the whole shebang.

Delays happen—it's how you handle and communicate about them

Full disclosure: The kind of delay I just described often...OK, basically always... happens with my major books. With *Out on the Wire*, the proposed contract said I'd deliver in 18 months. I knew when I got the contract that this deadline was unrealistic. I'd gone through this often enough. But my agent counseled me to go ahead and sign, so I did. Then, a year in, my editor was looking to schedule the book, and I had to renegotiate. I would have liked to have two more years, but she could only give me one. So I finished in an eight-month-long sprint, on time (according to the revised timeline). I don't really recommend this sprint method generally, but in this instance, it did mean that I got more time, and I did not get enough more time to waste any. It set the bar really high, and I cleared it.

But the bigger takeaway with this example is that the reason I was able to get additional time was that I was willing and able to communicate those needs to my editor with a lot of lead time. I relayed to her *six months ahead of the original contracted deadline* that I needed to adjust the calendar for the project, then worked with her to come up with a new timeline. While the resulting timeline was a compromise and a challenge for me, it was a much better result than what might have happened if I'd waited until Month 17 or 18 (i.e., close to the contracted deadline) to have the same conversation about the delay.

The same rules of thumb apply even when the only negotiating you're doing is with yourself.

Creative work sometimes does not happen on a schedule—and you can't make it. There are times you just have to accept that and make either the world, or your expectations, bend to that reality.

You may not be able to actually complete five pages of comics in a week, no matter how essential you deem it. Particularly right out of the gate, you may not even know what your work pace is. But as you develop, and *track*, your progress, you'll start to know yourself better. You'll get faster with practice, but you'll also get better at estimating how long a task will actually take you. Your job is to expand your capacity, but also gradually bring your expectations in line with what your capacity actually is.

As you get better at this, you may want to extend your planning timeline. But planning too far out means you'll almost always make major mistakes. You just can't see that far into the future.

What happened with the hypothetical cartoonist?

As our cartoonist friend went through her six-week plan, unfinished tasks piled up, and the last week was a bear. Week 6 was such a slog, she had to readjust her availability for the remaining creative work by calling in sick to work one day, and not talking to her mom at all. But she finished, which is a major accomplishment, and she had a great chat at the comics convention with the publisher, who seemed to really like her book.

Also, during the same six-week period, she talked to her mom seven times and had lunch with her twice. That fell far short of her specific, concrete calendar goals, but it was still twice as much contact as she and her mom had had in the previous six weeks, and it showed in the improvement in their relationship.

And her next six weeks?

Next time, our pal will realize that doing 16 pages, plus a cover and production, is just a bit too much to take on in only six weeks. She's got a better sense of what kind of time it really takes to do her work, and she'll adjust the timeline on future works so she doesn't run into that kind of crunch at the end. Meanwhile, she's got some orders for her book to fulfill.

You can find a goal-tracking model in the Workbook.

Activity:
Six-week goal tracking

Find this activity and any relevant worksheets
in the Growing Gills Workbook at http://jessicaabel.com/gg-reader.

Step 1. Start with the end: Name your goal for the next six weeks. Identify how you'll know you've achieved that goal.

Step 2. List phases that lead to achieving that goal.

Step 3. Name some metrics: What are your development markers for this goal? How will you know if you're on track or not? A vague sense of "I'm making work" or "I'm not making work" is highly unreliable. Can you come up with better benchmarks? How many hours a week do you have available for this work?

Step 4. Once you have an idea of all the steps involved in meeting your six-week goal, break them down to weeklong chunks and put them on a goal-tracking document. Once you do that, if you've been very diligent and vigilant in evaluating your proposed calendar, the most dangerous weeks that include far more than you can finish in one week should and will become immediately obvious. Avoid setting yourself up for failure and making yourself miserable: If you see now that there is no way you're achieving those goals in one week, readjust your calendar *or your expectations*.

Step 5. Re-evaluate what you list as single actions and ask yourself if that's accurate or if they are actually projects with multiple actions embedded within them. For any that are projects (e.g., "draft the conclusion"), build in

Quota action steps to get you to the finish line, and if it's likely to be very difficult, schedule in a couple of focus sessions (see Chapter 17) as well. They will accelerate your progress.

Step 6. Identify what dilemmas you must face to complete this work. Name the specific trade-offs, and make an agreement with yourself over what you will, and won't, give up to achieve your goal.

IMPORTANT: If you find yourself wanting to port over your entire "trusted system" to this tracking document, every phone call and email and to-do, **stop**. This tracking document is not for day-to-day use. It's a once-a-week review/overview. Your daily tasks (including the ones you're tracking on this doc) should be in your normal system. **This tracking sheet is a review document that gives you the 10,000-foot view of where you intend to be, and where you actually are.**

Chapter 16
The Long View
Finding the long-term vision for your creative life

If you're reading this, it's because when the going got tough around Chapter 7 and you easily could have dropped off, scary or not, you hung on to the fact that you've got big goals and hopes for your future. Even if you can't fully let yourself embrace that fact, yet.

And why is it so hard to embrace? Why do big, ambitious goals feel dangerous? Because admitting that you care is opening yourself up to failure. And you've been burned before.

I'm with you there. When I don't achieve my goals, I blame myself. I think "I didn't work hard enough" and recommit myself to work even harder next time.

I'm constantly hearing people say that the secret to creative success is "doing the work." Butt in chair. I've even kind of waffled on this myself, saying in one place that it's not as simple as all that, while elsewhere saying that the key is thinking less and making more.

But the real secret to creative success is defining "success." For yourself.

You can work like a burro, head down and pushing through, day in and day out, and never seem to get anywhere.

> **That's because simply working harder is not the answer; the key is working on the *right thing*.** 🖋

In order to clearly define what that "thing" is, sometimes you have to spend time envisioning your future projects. More to the point, you have to envision your future SELF.

Who do you want to be in the future? And are your current efforts leading you there?

Here's the truth: Of everything I've written about leading a creative life and improving creative productivity, this chapter is the one that talks most clearly about what holds ME back.

Lack of clarity on where I wanted to be—and lack of planning about how to get there—basically define my adult life.

You want examples? I've got 'em.

When it comes to finishing projects I set out to complete, I turned a corner a long time ago, and for at least the last 10 years, actually getting the work done has not been the problem.

The problem was—and is—which work?

Writing this chapter has made me think of a minimum of four or five major life phases I went through during which I devoted myself to some project, which I in fact finished, but it was the wrong project. "Wrong," meaning that having completed the project, I realized I had pointed myself in a misguided direction, so ended up not having met any goals I actually cared about.

Here's a specific example: As recently as two summers ago, I spent untold hours hand-drawing a GIF animation for a book trailer for the release of my book *Trish Trash* in the French market, thinking that it would help the book... somehow. However, they don't make book trailers in France, and therefore no one is accustomed to seeing book trailers. And I had absolutely no strategy about how I would get it distributed. I guess I sort of thought the publisher would see the book trailer and be so impressed, they'd run with it.

They didn't.

In fact, the book trailer has been seen by virtually no one. You can see it now if you like: It's on my *Trish Trash* webpage, and the soundtracked version (The music? *Not* picked by yours truly) is on YouTube. The latter has 139 views. Yep.

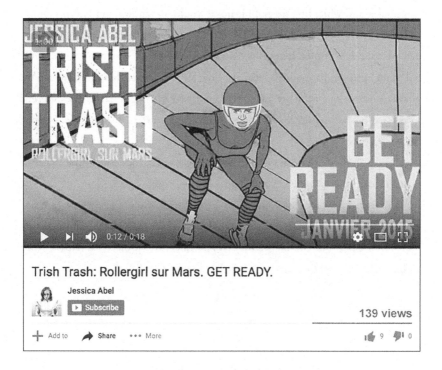

Mind you, I'm happy with how the clip came out creatively. This is why defining what constitutes "success" is so important. My book trailer did nothing toward the goal of getting my book noticed and getting people interested in buying it. That made it an enormous waste of energy irrespective of the quality of the clip, and the opportunity cost was immense: I spent my summer vacation drawing this thing all the while feeling rushed and "busy" instead of enjoying my summer. That's just dumb.

Identifying your primary goal and metric of success in a project is crucial. For example, if my primary goal had been to sell a lot of books, even making the *Out on the Wire* podcast, which I'm incredibly proud of and very glad I made for a whole variety of reasons, could be seen as a huge waste of energy. The podcast didn't sell very many books, and it took almost all of my time for over six months. As it is, among other things, the podcast enabled me to expand my storytelling skills immensely and build bridges with the audio world that I never would have had otherwise. Those bridges have led to opportunities to speak and lead workshops that have been both creatively and financially rewarding.

I'm not even going to tell you about how I vaguely hoped that drawing a 250-page black-and-white literary graphic novel would somehow lead to my becoming able to support myself as an author. Don't get me wrong: I would never want to not have created *La Perdida*. It's changed my life for the better in so many ways. But if I'd thought things through and realized how unlikely it was that this book would make a positive change in my financial circumstances, I might have made different choices about what else I was doing to build a viable career during those—count 'em—six years.

The lesson here is simple: Life goals are bigger than individual projects, even when those projects are really, really big.

This is the key to understanding why finishing some amazing project can ultimately feel so disappointing. Your goal was "finish the project," and you may not have figured out the bigger why. WHY finish the project? What is it for? What is the life goal that this project builds toward? ⭐

What happens when you don't think stuff through

What happens when you don't think that stuff through—what happened to me—is that you get to the end of a long project feeling proud and happy about the thing itself, but puzzled and disappointed that whatever change you thought would have magically happened as a result of completing that project (money, fame, attention, access, love, whatever), didn't.

And what often happens then—at least this is what happened for me—is that you plunge straight into the next project because all you can think to do is to keep working, working more and harder, and hoping that somehow the quality of the hard work you're doing will be noticed—somehow—eventually.

The longer that goes on, the more embittered you may feel, and that's what will make you want to stop doing the work. Which is no good.

My point is not to talk you out of doing work that isn't going to make you a bunch of money. I sincerely want you to make whatever work you want to make.

My point is to help you get clear about your larger goals, and then figure out if and how the work you have in front of you builds toward those goals.

It gives me immense satisfaction to help creative people build the life they want to build.

The question is, what life do you want to build?

Envisioning your future projects may be holding you back, but envisioning your future *self* is the key to becoming that self.

How can you set the right goals?

When you're drowning in Idea Debt, your main goal is (and should be) simply to do *something*, to build a creative practice of any kind. But when you sit down to work, you're likely to be distracted and scattered, unable to choose among the many options for how to spend your limited time.

In Chapter 8, I dispensed some relatively simple, tactical approaches to deciding which goal you should spend your energy on. But that activity assumes the right choice is already sitting on your list.

If you're not clear where you're going with your creative work, you really can't know if you're spending your one and only precious life in a way that will lead you to a sense of accomplishment and contentment...or not.

What role should creative work play in your life?

Questions to consider in determining the role creative work has in your life overall include:

- Is it what keeps you sane? Do you just need to do it?
- Is it meant to be paying your bills?
- Is it a means to an end? And if so, what is that end?

And then get more specific in terms of your chosen artistic genres and formats:

- Do you want to make comics? Or do you want to have lots of people read your comics? Or do you want to make a living as a cartoonist?
- Do you want to have a deeper knowledge of your area of study? Or do you want to get a faculty job?
- Do you want to make a podcast? Or do you want to be a professional podcaster?
- Do you want writing to be a part of your daily life? Or do you want to have a large, passionate audience for your writing? Or do you want to build

relationships with other writers? Or do you want to be a full-time writer?

- Do you want to paint and have others appreciate your work? Or do you want to quit your day job to devote yourself to painting?

Let me emphasize, these are all completely valid choices. However, they're completely *different* choices.

For example: While making a living as a cartoonist will definitely include making comics, there may be a lot less of this than you might imagine and a lot more entrepreneurship, including building your audience, marketing, and sales.

If you want to make comics that are read by a huge number of people, but you're not that concerned with making a living at it, you may make totally different choices about how you publish and how you build your connections with your audience. You also may end up making a living at it. But then again, you might not, if you're not focused on that outcome.

If your goal is to be able to afford to quit your day job to paint, simply working harder and getting better at painting will not get you there.

For the most part, hard work and good work are the cost of entry. But harder work and more work will not create exponentially better results.

The key to achieving your goals is defining and then envisioning your future success in a very specific, detailed way...and then using that vision to build a plan that will get you there.

How to use future-you
to guide your present choices

I call the activity that follows the Vision Quest, because I wanted to choose a name that you'll have a hard time taking seriously. Laughter and anxiety don't cohabitate well.

This activity is about honoring future-you, and what future-you wants to be doing. Think of it like NASA planning to explore Mars. It takes 20+ years of preparation to get there.

The idea for this process came from Louise, a student in the Creative Focus Workshop who was struggling to figure out what she wanted to be working on:

I get stuck because I don't know which body of work I most want to build. Fiction? Nonfiction? Play? Film? And for the two that DO seem to build toward something, my big question is what genre they should be.

What struck me was that Louise was giving all the options equal weight, as though they were completely interchangeable. That led to Shiny Object Syndrome, in which as soon as she started to decide on one thing, she'd be distracted by another. So I challenged her as follows:

Can you do a thought experiment for this?

Imagine yourself in 10 years, having built this body of work (whatever it is) with 2 to 5 major projects, and any number of smaller bits and pieces. See who you come into contact with professionally around it. Imagine what kinds of creative work and research you're engaged in. Imagine you're successful with it—which conferences will you attend? Which awards do you want to win? What relationship do you want with your audience? All of that is very different depending on which way you go. How do you want to feel in your skin projecting way out into the future?

Once she took this advice and imagined a more specific future self, it was immediately apparent to her that she wanted to work among journalists because that's who she considered her "tribe." So the work wasn't all equivalent after all.

This is the problem: In the moment, you want to be immersed in the work, to lose yourself in it. But before you do that, you've got to exercise conscious choice over what you're going to devote all that energy to. You need to pull back and think about how this choice fits into your big picture.

Once Michael, whom we first met in Chapter 8, completed the One Goal he set in the Creative Focus Workshop, he started to get an inkling of what he was actually capable of. But in order to decide what his next project should be, he needed to know what his big-picture goals were, so he could set out in the right direction. To think that through, Michael worked through the Vision Quest activity, below.

This is about having a vision for the very long range. In the workshop we had the 6-week cycle. And now, we're imagining what might be in five years, that's a whole different range. Having done the workshop and the six-week tracking thing, I knew what was doable and could extrapolate for five years. I realized, Hey, the dream I've had for a long time of having an anthology of my own, and contributing stories to other publications, that's within the range of the possible!

My current goal is to get back into the habit of reading fiction (I have not read fiction—other than comic books—in years) and preparing to write stories. (Writing a story is still a terrifying task for me, so I'll take this slow.) At the end of my current 6-week plan I expect to have an outline of a new story in terms of premise, theme, characters and action.

My long-term goal (as seen in the Vision Quest process) is to regularly create and publish short comic book stories, to contribute to anthologies, and to publish an anthology of my own.

Activity:
Vision Quest

Step 1. Sit down with your Vision Quest worksheet and your Idea Debt list, and think about each of the main interests reflected in the list. What would your life be like if you focused on only that category of thing for the next five years?

Step 2. Now, imagine yourself five years from now, having built your defining body of work (whatever it is) with two to five major projects, and any number of smaller bits and pieces.

Questions to Consider:

Who will you be working with? Who are your colleagues and peers? What kinds of personal and professional qualities should they have? Can you name actual individuals you would like to see shift from being people you admire to being your colleagues?

What kind of world will you move in, and at what level? Do you want to be a passionate amateur, a devotee, a journeyman professional, or at the top of the game? What kind of conferences and professional events would you go to, and in what capacity? Are there awards or acknowledgments you want to win?

What relationship will you build with an audience around your work? Are you seeking an enormous public audience; an intimate, intense audience; or a few select clients? How do you want them to think of your work? What role will it play in their lives?

What income, if any, will you derive from creative work? Do you want this to be your job? Is the work at the center of your professional life, or is it just one component of a bigger picture? What other compensation do you want? Time? Recognition? The pure enjoyment of creating?

(**NOTE:** If making money with your work is something you want to aim for, it needs to be a specific goal. Making creative work into a career, or even an important income-stream producer, takes its own kind of creativity, as well as time and effort. If this is a goal, you can't spend all your time making the work and neglect building the career side.)

How will you spend your days? What does your workspace look like? Full time, or part time? Working with staff, or alone? Employed by someone or freelance? How much travel? How much admin as opposed to creating?

How do you want to feel in your skin?

Step 3. Use the answers to the preceding questions to imagine that future-you as fully as you can. Define (and write down) specific benchmarks that will mark "success" to you.

Step 4. Ask yourself if the work you're doing today is what you need to be doing to achieve that vision. What happens if you *don't* focus on projects and goals that lead to a single vision, but instead spread your efforts over many interests? Where does that put you in five years?

Step 5. Think through what your real goals are with the Vision Quest worksheet, and then reassess your One Goal to make sure you've picked the right one for you.

Part 4:
Falling Down &
Getting Up

What we're doing in this section

In most other books about creative productivity, you'd be finished now. At this point, you've got your lists and plans and calendars all made, and you've thought through your vision for five years down the line. What more can we say? But I am a cartoonist and writer myself, and I know from experience there are things that will stop you that have nothing to do with making lists. I wanted to make sure we talk about a few of those things in this last section, and to give you a few more tools to tackle some of the big issues we all face.

What you'll achieve in Part 4:

- Identify, and discover techniques to escape, the Dark Forest.
- Master tools to overcome resistance.
- Create a restart plan for emergencies when you're completely overwhelmed.

Chapter 17
The Dark Forest
Why and how we go through creative crisis in the midst of big projects, and some ways to escape it

There you are, skipping down the path, making your work—let's say it's a novel. The sun is shining, birds are chirping, you feel great. You. can. do this.

You've got your map (your trusted system) to guide you, you know the chronology of what's ahead of you on the path. You write a scene, and then another. But as you get deeper into it, you start asking yourself..."is this the right way?" You find yourself at the edge of the woods.

Questions and doubts start to creep up on you. Why does this character act this way? Does this setup make any sense? Why does this guy show up here? Wait, does any of this mean anything?

You see a wall of words, just all this *stuff*. You're not blocked, you're the opposite of blank, but you've got no sense of what's better than anything else. You've got no way to grapple with or evaluate the material you've produced.

Suddenly you notice that those lovely trees that bordered the path have grown tall all around you, blocking out the sun. Wind starts whipping through the branches. Every direction seems equally perilous. There's no longer a clear way forward. You're lost.

Welcome to the forest.

I got the metaphor of the forest from Jad Abumrad of *Radiolab*, who talked about his own walk in the darkness at the Third Coast Audio Fest:[*]

> *The station manager came to me and he said "Hey, do you want to do an hour on Wagner's Ring Cycle?" And I thought to myself, OK. Wagner, Wagner, Wagner, I don't know much about Wagner. But, uh, sure OK, Wagner, why not.*
>
> *Fast forward a couple months, I had missed four deadlines, I'm on the verge of getting fired, and I haven't slept for four days. I had the pressure of ideas that were just out of reach. It was awful.*
>
> *And we at Radiolab have given this state of mind a name, because it happens quite often. We call it the German forest.*

The German Forest. That image resonated for me all too strongly. Because when I talked to Jad, it was the fall of 2013, and I was in the midst of trying to write *Out on the Wire*, and it was not going well.

When you get lost in those deep, dark woods, you think you're crazy. You think that no one has ever felt this before. And the fact that you're feeling it must mean that you aren't any good at this work, and you can't do it.

In August 2012, I had done the interview that appears below with Robert Smith and Zoe Chace at *Planet Money*. But then, over a year later, as I struggled to figure out what my book was really about, I found myself re-listening to it.

Interview with Robert Smith and Zoe Chace

Robert: There will always be a moment where we think...

Zoe: ...it's a bad idea

Robert: We'll say it out loud. Why did we volunteer in the meeting? We thought it was exciting.

Zoe: Should we throw this away?

Robert: Should we ditch it? The tape's not good, the idea's not good. We doubt

---

[*] *http://thirdcoastfestival.org/explore/feature/these-are-a-few-of-jad-abumrads-favorite-things*

our own excitement. And then you find it again, you find the thing that got you excited in the first place.

Me: *I think that's the nature of writing, though. That happens to me with every project multiple times because they usually take me about three years...*

Robert: *You want to write out a postcard right now that I can send you in six months that says, "I'm really, I'm excited about this story."? To your future self.*

Listening to that interview again in the fall of 2013 when I felt lost was like I *really had* sent myself that postcard. This is what I wrote that day: "I knew this would happen, I knew it's gonna feel really shitty. Like, you can't breathe like you're getting fat like you're losing brain cells like you will never be able to think about anything else ever again like there is no end to the German forest."

There are no periods in that sentence!

I read that sentence out loud to my podcast producer Benjamin Frisch in a story meeting, and I literally got choked up. It sucks to be in the Dark Forest. Rereading my thoughts from that time out loud just put me, bang, right back in that emotional place.

So what the hell is the Dark Forest?

The Dark Forest is where you end up when you're way out on the wire.

It's when you're sitting down to do the work, but it's so difficult, and the work comes so slowly, that you just can't believe that you could possibly be doing it right. It's not that you aren't working; in fact, that's almost become part of the problem. You've created so much that the thread you started off with is now a messy tangle of wool.

Behind closed doors, you're asking yourself questions that may never have crossed your mind when you started:

- Is this it? Because this doesn't feel great. Isn't it supposed to feel great when I'm actually writing?
- Am I really cut out for this? Does this mean I have no talent?

- Do I have it in me to finish this project?

- Is my idea actually any good?

- Is it time to give up?

The bad news is: This is often what it feels like to make art. It can feel like you're flailing, like you're completely incapable of getting your mind all the way around the subject at hand.

Kazu Kibuishi, who came up with the Idea Debt concept, is a genuine, honest-to-god, highly successful narrative artist. He's author of the graphic novel series, and recently announced film, *Amulet*. But the fact that he's a bestselling, many-times-published author isn't enough to keep him out of the woods. He wrote an extremely popular tweet that summed up his experience of making the work. This tweet is, in fact, *why* I interviewed him, and how Kazu happened to have the opportunity to blow my little mind with Idea Debt.

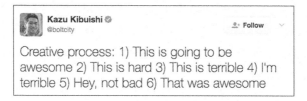

No. 4 on that list? "I'm terrible"? That's what hurts the most. But it wasn't true about Kazu, it's not true about you, and it's not true about me.

Day to day, I hit moments when I think: "I don't know if I can figure this out!" But when you're in the forest, that struggle becomes bigger and tips over into thinking, "I can't figure this out...because I'm stupid and ugly and a complete failure as a human being."

That's not just self-doubt. That's self-hatred. It's shame, stemming from feeling that you're not good enough to handle the job you've set yourself, that now everyone will know how useless you are.

And frankly, some of the other steps in the middle? They do not necessarily go so smoothly or so chronologically. It could go something like this:

This is terrible.

This is OK.

I'm terrible.

This is hard.

This is OK.

This is awesome.

I am terrible. God I'm so stupid, I am an idiot. I will never make it out of this. I will never ever see the light of day again.

Oh, I see how this might come together.

No. I don't. AAAAAH!!!

This is not writer's block. Or at least it's not the Hollywood version of writer's block, in which you don't put a word on paper, and you loll by the pool, chain-smoking and drinking martinis while your agent tries to track you down.

No, what I'm describing is much more akin to writing words and words and words and words and words until you're swimming in words, and none of them make any sense to you. At that point, continuing feels futile because no idea feels any better than any other idea, and how would you know anyway, you're such an idiot.

That's where I was that fall of 2013, as I was writing *Out on the Wire*:

I've bitten off way more than I can chew. All I've got to show for over a year of research and logging and writing is a file of over 200,000 words, in a vague order, with no narration written by me.

That's the pivotal moment.

The Dark Forest changes you

Whenever you're making a large, complex work of any kind, so many moving parts go into it. Every ambitious project has many conceptual parts and many technical parts, and at some point you have to have taken all those things in, but you haven't put them in order yet.

The putting-it-in-order process is a whole phase of the work, and a very important one. That dip in the middle of the process, from "I'm terrible" to "Hey, not bad" looks like a simple step, but it's actually a huge leap. The thinking process that you go through in that period of a project—and sometimes it's a technical process as well, if you have to master a skill in order to get there—that is where you grow.

That takes deliberate practice. That's where you get better as an artist, and that's where the work becomes something unique in the world. If you don't hit that point with a project, there's nothing wrong with it, but it probably means this project may not be the deepest thing that you've ever done. It may not be breaking new ground for you or for anybody else. If you really want to break new ground, you're going to have to go through the Dark Forest. *necessary*!

Here's me again, struggling with the entire point of the *Out on the Wire* book project:

> *And every time I read over my notes on an interview, or watch a video of these people talking, I just want to go back and spend more time talking to them, and listening to them. They're so smart and thoughtful. Why even do this book? I'll just give you a list of streaming audio links, and you'll do fine.*

Fortunately for me, all that tape I was struggling with? It was full of insights from the most creative, most productive people in the world. They've been through this Dark Forest, too. And they found their way out.

How others get out of the forest

The first thing I learned is that everyone goes through this—and to get out of the Dark Forest, you've got to go deeper in. Stephanie Foo of *This American Life* put it best when she said, *"...you might not feel like it's working...but that's what it takes. That's what everybody goes through to become good."*

Jay Allison of *The Moth Radio Hour* gave me my second clue: to work through it, you need to immerse yourself and get deeply into the flow of the story:

To me, that's the joy and pain of the work. Getting deep into a story and figuring out, How do I keep this moving, how do I keep the balls in the air. How do I advance all my armies down the field, and the more complex it gets, the more complex it gets.

There's a great peace in this work because you can't multitask. It's the one time I have to shut everything else off, because you can only exist in the flow of your story, because if you don't, you're going to miss something, you're not going to be far enough into it.

...to get that deep, to get as deep as you need to get to make it transcendent...

It's still just enervating, I don't know how to do this, can't make it as good as I should...and I think that's why a lot of people stop creative work, because it's too hard.

This moment is when most people just stop, and switch to some other project. Following your work as deep as it needs to go takes an iron constitution. You've got to truly trust yourself and the tools and skills you've learned or are learning, even when the forest makes everything feel wrong.

And the fact is, you might actually BE wrong. Here's a third clue: When you're in the forest, you've got to be ready to deploy the dynamite. Joe Richman of *Radio Diaries* told me he's always ready to blow up his structure and start over:

Have a structure before you even go out, even if you blow it up. But have an idea of what the beginning is, the ending. What the piece is about.

The more you can draw a map early and then continue to redraw as you go the better off. Because what's dangerous is to have all this tape and then you get there and it's just completely overwhelming and frightening and you have no idea what you're doing. You have to kind of pretend to know what you're doing, sometimes.

I struggled with a mountain of tape for eight months before I knew what my story was for *Out on the Wire*. I wandered in search of the story.

I had a notion what it was about, but then blew it up. I rewrote my structure radically four times, and in some ways ended up exactly where I started.

I had to fight my way through.

OK, that's all well and good. But isn't there a better way to escape the Forest than just slogging through it?

Escape from the Dark Forest!
The Focus Session

The secret to accelerating your escape from the darkness is editorial collaboration. If you talk to someone about what you're trying to achieve, and you try to explain the bits that are slipping away from you, you'll start to find the answers you need.

And if you record your conversations, you'll have a way to hold on to those insights.

Céline was working on an autobiographical audio story about how she turned her life upside down in order to care for two baby wild boars on her father's remote farm in Germany. She'd written a really powerful Story Matrix (a story structure tool I talk about in Episode 4 of the *Out on the Wire* podcast) in which she created parallels between her own decision-making vis-à-vis the boars and her father's reckless behavior, which had always stood between them:

> *Céline is determined to never let anybody get too close to her, especially her father, who somehow always ends up hurting her. But then during a visit to her father's farm, an orphan wild baby boar named Gustav decides to adopt Céline as his replacement mom...Like everybody else, she knows from the beginning that raising a male wild boar is a stupid and possibly dangerous idea, but she can't help it.*

The idea was heartfelt, original, and profound. It had also landed Céline deep in the Dark (German) Forest, both literally and metaphorically.

One of Céline's wild baby boars. OMG, I would seriously consider throwing over my whole life for a little guy like this, too. Photo by Céline Keller

Céline was a member of the *Out on the Wire* Working Group, the online community associated with the *Out on the Wire* podcast for workshopping our stories. But after being a constant presence in the group for a month, she'd disappeared. I was riveted by her story about the boars, and I noticed her absence. But I had a feeling I knew what was going on: The Dark Forest had closed in on her.

My producer Benjamin Frisch and I had just finished an episode of the podcast on the Dark Forest*. We were looking for a way to do a workshop episode that would really get at the heart of what the Forest felt like, and how to get out. So we decided to call Céline, and we held a Focus Session on the podcast.

> **The secret of getting out of the Forest isn't "doing the work," it's a Focus Session.**

Sure enough, when we reached Céline, it turned out she was indeed trapped in the Forest. She felt tied to her original idea, and it was sinking her. She had lost her initial excitement. I believe she was in danger of actually abandoning her project, which would have been a shame. Her interest in the subject of wild boars, which are in crisis in Germany, only grew stronger with every passing day—every time she read a new report or found a new organization devoted to them. But because

---

* *http://jessicaabel.com/podcast/episode-7-dark-forest*

her original idea centered on her relationship with her father, the time she spent investigating the larger issues made her feel like she was in some way betraying her story. Meanwhile, her father wouldn't be caught on tape, and she hated how her own diary audio sounded.

Benjamin and I reassured her that the new direction was not only OK but a positive development. Yes, this new story direction meant she'd need to work up the courage to interview scientists and other experts, including local hunters who might see her as critical. Strangers. But the burst of energy Céline felt from realizing that she was not wrong, that she knew in her gut what her story should really be, will sustain her as she tries new things.

Céline left the conversation feeling really good about her work, and so her story is that much closer to actually existing in the world. Which is good for all of us. It's a story I want to hear, and, believe me, you do, too.

The actual German forest with the actual German boars. Not as scary as in my imagination…
Photo by Céline Keller

Ask for help from others
when you need it

So many times in my life, I've had this experience: The knowledge required to make the next step is in me, somewhere. I know it is. I can feel it in there, trying to get out. But I just can't grasp it.

That's when you need to reach out for help. You may feel shame that you don't have better control of your work, especially if you're a pro, but this is an incredibly common experience. It takes guts to allow yourself to be vulnerable, to admit you feel lost in the big, scary Dark Forest. It's an act of bravery that comes from caring deeply about the work and about yourself.

Open up to a friend or colleague and say, "I don't know what I'm doing here. I feel like I'm drowning, like I've got all these things, all these ideas floating around, and I need to put them in some order, but I don't understand. Let me try to explain this to you."

We all live with a sort of amnesia about the creative process, forgetting that the "I'm terrible" phase comes just three short steps after "This is going to be awesome." It's a good amnesia to have, in the sense that if you could remember vividly how painful "I'm terrible" feels, you might never create anything. But we don't have to have amnesia about the way out of the pit. That's why I give the tools I've found to have worked concrete names, like "Focus Session," and packaged them up in worksheets. It's another reminder that practical techniques and solutions to the problems you are encountering exist. Next time you're lost out there, just try to remember, there's a worksheet for this.

The second I sit down with someone to talk things through (usually with Matt, but not always), that knowledge starts to bubble up. I talk through what I'm thinking, what I'm struggling with, and before I know it, I've got clarity. Often, I don't even really need advice at all. I just need to put myself in a situation in which I have to clearly explain my problem to someone else. Here's what that looked like for one of my Dark Forest moments during writing *Out on the Wire*:

> *Jessica: I'm struggling, and you are too, I'm struggling with, what is the difference between these things?*
>
> *Matt: Maybe each chapter needs a title...*
>
> *Jessica: Focus sentence for each chapter.*
>
> *Matt: Focus sentence for each chapter.*

I don't mean to say that by the end of every such conversation, I've got the whole thing (whatever it is) written. But I have unwound some complicated relationship between characters, I've spotted the flaw in my logic, I've figured out how to say something subtle...And above all, I know what I need to do next.

Which is to write.

And then that's what I do, instead of just sitting there staring at my screen for hours, days, weeks.

Keep in mind also that getting lost in the Dark Forest can happen repeatedly on a project, so you may need many of those conversations with another person to help you emerge and get back to work. Matt and I talked about every page, every concept, every connection in *Out on the Wire*, all the way through that fall of 2013, as I grappled with the deepest and darkest Forest I'd ever gotten lost in. Each time we did, I felt another ray of sunshine break through the gloom.

This is a Focus Session.

This is not just having coffee. It's not "support." It's a *system* for feedback and collaborative improvement. It's reliable, it's repeatable. I don't wait for inspiration or luck. I hate waiting for luck. Luck is always late.

If you're stuck in the Dark Forest, try a Focus Session, and see if you can't build a catapult to help you escape.

Activity: Focus Session

Find this activity and any relevant worksheets in the Growing Gills Workbook at http://jessicaabel.com/gg-reader.

Step 1. Assess your collaborator. You don't need to find a pro, just someone who would be a great reader/viewer/listener for your finished work. It should be someone who is willing to spend an hour imaginatively entering fully into your project. That means someone who knows how to listen, who can be attentive to you and to details, and who is open enough to go where you want to go.

Step 2. Set the stage, part 1: Ask for a specific amount of time. It's a lot easier to say yes to "Can I bend your ear for an hour?" than "I really need your help on this project I'm stuck on." That can feel overwhelming.

Step 3. Set the stage, part 2: Decide what kind of feedback you want. Do you just want someone to listen? Do you want to get their take on what you're trying to communicate? Do you want to brainstorm new ideas? Give your collaborator the worksheet and discuss your expectations before you start.

Step 4. Meet in person, or at least over a video call. (If possible, avoid a dialogue that's only audio. You want to be able to read the other person's face.) Ideally, make it a bit fun. Make lunch or invite the person out. Buy your collaborator coffee at a favorite place, or have a glass of wine.

Step 5. RECORD! Record the whole conversation on a pocket recorder, and then listen to the tape again later to take notes and extract more ideas from the session.

If you want to hear an example of this in action, you can listen to our actual Focus Session with Céline in the *Out on the Wire* workshop episode 7.5.[*]

Why do we have to visit the Dark Forest?

The truly amazing thing is, you do get through it. I got through it, and everyone I interviewed has gotten through it, over and over. You think it's never going to happen, and then it happens.

Jad Abumrad from *Radiolab* did eventually finish that Wagner piece:

When I heard the thing on the radio later, I was like, "oh, somewhere in the middle of that trauma, I think I found my voice."

It is one of the first times when I heard myself on the radio and thought, "oh yeah, I could work with that. I see where that guy is going. And I kinda want to go there with him."

There's a real correlation—to use the science word—between time spent in the

---

[*] *http://jessicaabel.com/podcast/workshop-7-5-dark-forest*

German Forest and these moments of emergence. That's what I believe.

I've been lost deep in the Dark Forest on every major project I've ever done. Even on smaller projects, I spend at least a few hours there.

I've been doing this creative work long enough that if I didn't get at least a little bit stuck in those brambles, I'd worry that I wasn't going far enough out on the wire. That feeling of being lost is what happens when your brain is working the hardest to make connections, to understand what this morass of work you've produced actually means. And if I'm not stretching? Maybe I'm not doing my best work.

The good news is, the projects in which you find yourself seriously lost like this are really only the big, important ones. This kind of stuck doesn't happen with little things, with easy, unchallenging work. If what you're doing is deep, if it's worth doing, it's going to be hard.

So when you're in the Dark Forest, be kind to yourself. It's impossible not to think, "Am I doing it wrong?" in these moments. Just try not to go all the way to "I'm terrible." Take a walk, take a shower, take a nap. Your mind is doing its work, and it hurts. But keep working, and you will escape from the forest. And there's a beautiful sunny glade on the other side.

It hurts because it really matters. It's complicated because it's full of ideas. It's hard because you're too close.

You'll emerge from the Dark Forest, and when you do, you'll be a new person. The forest is fire, and it's that fire that will forge you into an artist.

Chapter 18
The Resistance (Not the Good Kind)
Facing and overcoming your own resistance
to making your work

Procrastination, when it passes a certain point, stops feeling like simply putting things off (as crappy as that feels) and starts to feel like creative block. I've talked a lot about the idea that procrastination stems from anxiety and feeds anxiety, and this is an extreme example. This game, of trying to create self-generated work, is not a physical battle, it's a psychological one. When you face what feels like block, your Should Monster goes wild, and the stakes feel higher and higher, resulting in less and less getting done.

I'm no shrink, but it's a pretty sure thing that your state of mind is feeding the problem. It's a Catch-22 situation. In order to make the work, you've got to chill out and forgive yourself, to find some equilibrium. In order to forgive yourself and relax, you may feel like you've got to start something, no matter how small. Deciding to take that action can then put you into a tailspin, your mind goes blank, and you're back to square one.

How to get out of this cycle?

Again, I'm not a professional at this, but in my personal experience, once you eliminate the immediate suspects—you haven't broken a project down to steps, so you don't know what to do next; you haven't identified your highest priorities, so you keep flipping from one thing to another; you haven't identified your dilemmas, so everything feels surprisingly hard; and so on—it's probably because some hidden emotion in there is tripping you up.

If you learn to identify when that seized-up feeling is coming, and feel that moment when you start to get squirrelly, you can stop what you're doing and just let yourself think about that feeling. Try to work backward. What was the specific word, thought, or action that triggered it? What happened there? A hidden emotion is in there, and there's a to-do item attached to it. Find it, and get it into your trusted system (even if the to-do is "have a hard conversation with my mom"), and you'll resolve the majority of that feeling. Knowing is so much better than not knowing.

You might feel resistance because the task will be hard for you, outside your comfort zone, and that's uncomfortable. Or it might be something that's late, and you feel guilty. It might be something you really don't want to do at all, ever, but you promised yourself or someone you would do it, and saying no now will be all that much more difficult. It might be that doing this task will put you in contact with people you don't want to deal with, or in a way you don't want to deal with them. Most of it breaks down to "fear about potential interpersonal unpleasantness" or "negative thoughts about yourself."

Most of these fears, while real, will wither to a much more manageable size when exposed to sunlight.

Activity:
Resistance analyzer

**Find this activity and any relevant worksheets
in the Growing Gills Workbook at http://jessicaabel.com/gg-reader.**

The key to moving past your block, as with making progress on giant projects we want to tackle, is in breaking it down:

Step 1: Do a little bit of meta-work on it. List some bits/ideas/tasks that need to go into it.

Step 2: Make a mind map of that. Don't do the things, just name them.

Step 3: When you come up against a phase or task that's making you want to run screaming, pause and sit there for a minute. Think about it. That thing is pushing some button, possibly one that isn't even related on the surface. See if you can locate it. Sometimes just naming it will make it ease up.

Step 4: Start by identifying the smallest possible action you can take to begin the project. This can be something as easy as "open the email and reread it" or even "find the email." Visualize how relieved and proud you'll be that you started (and finished?) a really hard thing.

Step 5: Schedule a reward you'll earn by finishing. A TV show, coffee out, a glass of something harder if need be...

What to do if you can't allow yourself to analyze your resistance

If even sitting with whatever may be blocking you from working and thinking about it feels too hard, try Lynda Barry's spirals. In *What It Is,* Lynda gives a free-writing exercise that's great for getting moving. But there are moments when you feel so empty, you can't pull a sentence together. She recommends drawing slow, careful spirals, allowing yourself to just be in the moment with your hand moving, until something comes into your mind. It's kind of like a drawing meditation.

Also, don't forget the other super-useful technique that you've learned for easing up the block: a Focus Session.

Chapter 19

Restart

Getting back on track when you've gotten derailed

I'm staring at the spinning beach ball of death.

My cache is full...

Need to quit some apps...

Time to restart.

You may not be finishing this book with a triumphant feeling. You may be overwhelmed and feel guilty that you're not doing more to take control. You may have basically never felt in control, and you can't imagine what that would be like.

When you're in that place, it's like you're stuck in a churning wheel of anxiety and pain, like you're in a hole and you can't get out. No matter what you're doing, it's the wrong thing, and then you switch to another task or technique, and that's the wrong thing, too... You are not alone. You are not weird, you are not broken. This feeling—that anywhere you are at present is the Wrong Place—is the most common experience I know.

Even if you deeply understand all the stuff I've thrown at you, no matter how awesome your focus and planning, you will fall off the horse. Everyone does. I do, and I'm literally writing the *book* about how to get your creative work done.

Here's me last fall:

I'm sitting in my shiny new office at my shiny new job, in front of a huge, blazing-fast new Mac. I have been away from the studio, from my workplace, all summer, and I have five courses to plan, an essay to write, most of a comic book to draw, a whole bunch of correspondence to write, and a blog post to finish. This blog post.

So what the hell am I doing browsing mini-fridges on Amazon?

The thought sequence that led me here: I like to drink tea. And in my tea, I like to have milk. In order to have milk at hand, I need refrigeration. I work on the 5th floor. The closest refrigerator is on the 3rd floor. I will never go to the 3rd floor just for milk.

Ipso facto.

I catch myself in the middle of the act of Amazon-ing, and a wave of disgust at my lack of focus sweeps over me. I open a document and stare at the words I've already typed. I flip to my email and answer a couple short things, skipping the hard ones. I get up to organize my books.

What! EVER!

Later that week, I read Charlie Gilkey, in his newsletter[*]:

The basic idea is that the longer you've been out of your routine, the longer it's going to take for you to transition out of and into it again. If you're gone longer than 30 days, you're likely into a new routine altogether; in short, you've developed a new normal, and getting into your "normal" home routine is going to take some adjustment.

Reading that gave me some perspective and got me out of the self-blame trap. Not only had I been out of the studio for eight weeks, I had purchased a house, gotten a job, and moved *countries*. There were reasons I was so out of whack. And it's not like I hadn't seen this coming a year out. Moving overseas, getting a job, setting up a new life, these changes don't happen by accident. They take a

[*] *http://www.productiveflourishing.com*

hell of a lot of planning, and I knew it would all be disruptive. I even planned time to be off-grid. But in the end, that didn't matter: The actual process of getting back in the rhythm, a new rhythm, is long and painful, and filled with self-loathing.

I'd been telling myself: "I'm finally back in a house. Sure, it's a new house, but at least I sleep in my own bed every night. I should be dying to get back to work." I told myself, "Really it's just that I have to commit to think."

As though it were just a matter of commitment, of *wanting it enough*.

If that were true, a lot more people out there would be making their life's work, instead of just dreaming about it.

It is not just a matter of commitment. Yes, you've got to commit. But willpower alone will not get you back on that horse. You need a methodology, something to hang on to when you feel like you'll never, ever, be able to focus again.

For me, at least, there is no black-belt level of regaining creative momentum. It's hard, every time. And it hurts. I hurt *myself* by thinking that if only I were smarter, better, and/or more in control, I wouldn't be feeling this way.

It's worth repeating: Procrastination is caused by anxiety...and procrastination causes anxiety. It's a cycle, a filthy trick.

Self-blame is not useful. Action is useful.

I needed a restart.

Regaining focus and creative momentum after getting derailed

I feel like the end of summer derails almost everyone: You take a vacation, go to too many barbecues, stay up late too many nights, and then before you know it, you're completely thrown off and behind on your creative work. This is especially true if you need to set your own deadlines and be self-motivated. If you have kids, they go back to school, and you're suddenly thrown into a new, intense schedule built around dropoffs and lunches and pickups.

But whether you've been off your rhythm for a couple of weeks or even for years, you can do a few things to try to regain control of your time and focus. You'll recognize these steps from earlier in the book. This is the express-version, the emergency-room, stanch-the-bleeding version:

Step 1:
Self-forgiveness

When you've got a tidal wave of undone stuff bearing down on you, you may feel helpless and overwhelmed. You may feel like there's nothing good in your life, like you're worthless. That feeling is contributing to the problem.

Step back, look at all the areas of your life, and assess when and where you're in control. Ask yourself, "Where is it that everything isn't collapsing around me? What's working? What am I proud of?"

Inevitably, you're handling something competently.

Have you paid your bills on time? Check.

Are you fed? Check.

Taking showers? Good for you.

Maybe you clean when you're procrastinating, and your house is sparkling. Kudos.

Maybe you just make sure to get to work on time.

Whatever it is, pat yourself on the back and meditate on it for a while to help change your point of view.

If you feel comfortable with asking yourself "What am I grateful for?" this is the time to write down answers to that one. Myself, I am still too much a cynical punk at heart to go there, but I'm trying.

When your Should Monster rears its ugly head and says you *should* be working, and if you're not, you're a piece of crap and will never dig out of this hole ever... just put a box around that and tell yourself, "This is normal. It's not *true*, but it's normal to feel this way. Everyone does. Even Jessica." That will help.

Step 2:
Survey the lay of the land

When you get back from a break, whether voluntary or involuntary, there's a drag effect on your ability to focus on a few levels:

- On the one hand, it's literal: If you've been away, you'll have more stacked-up tasks.
- Then there's the fact that you're simply out of the habit of concentration.

The first drag will resolve itself after a while and get back to whatever your normal level of chaos is. The second drag is actually the harder of the two to deal with, though when resolved, it will certainly help with the first!

You need to take stock of your commitments, to yourself and to others. Your open loops are scattered all over the place. You've got to gather them up. What have you explicitly or implicitly promised to do?

When you don't know the answer to this, everything feels urgent.

Activity:
Restart

**Find this activity and any relevant worksheets
in the Growing Gills Workbook at http://jessicaabel.com/gg-reader.**

Step 1. Clean your desk. This step applies to whatever your "desk" is, even if it's a backpack. Include all the places you've done work or left notes or messages to yourself: your kitchen table, refrigerator magnets, table by the door, coffee table. Clean it up, and each time you find something that calls out to you to deal with it, write down what you're supposed to do with that thing. Cleaning can feel like procrastination (and it might be!), but I give you permission, if you need it, to do this first.

Step 2. Categorize your list, dividing "Must" from "Would Like To," and "Now" from "Can Wait."

This is not quite the same as the Pressing-Vital idea. This is emergency triage.

Before you go further, be honest: Does everything in the "Must" bucket really belong there? Or is your Should Monster telling you things you really would like to do are Musts? Even really big important creative projects are often "would like to." That's important to acknowledge because it means that when we devote time to that work, it's a positive choice. When we don't do it, that's a choice as well, not victimization.

Next steps after the restart activity

Congratulations: You've now effectively slashed the number of items your anxious brain needs to bounce around all the time.

Anything that's in the Can Wait bucket, you can safely put off, and temporarily ignore until you're ready to devote a bit of time to going through the full planning process described in Parts 1 and 2 of this book.

Anything that is in both the Must + Now buckets, just do that stuff. (Easier said than done. Read on.)

How to tackle the Must + Now list:

Calendar the small stuff. If it's small, get it on your calendar, and make it so. Usually, this part of the list—if you're honest—is not that long, or if it is long, it's mostly made up of petty admin tasks: emails you need to answer, paperwork. Annoying but easy tasks. Get blocks of time on your calendar and think through the trade-offs of completing those tasks. Then write an agreement with yourself to commit to those trade-offs. For me, irritating and lengthy administrative tasks—opening 16 apps to gather info, logging into 12 web portals, locating passwords—will stop me in my tracks if I don't acknowledge what it will take to complete them.

Reset deadlines where possible. If this part of the list includes items that involve collaborators or clients, assess whether you can push back the deadlines. Communicate with them about your schedule as early as you can.

Break down the big projects into doable tasks, as small as you can manage. If some of the list items are large and unwieldy, they are probably projects, not tasks. So make sure to break them down into the tiniest steps you can imagine and then add them to your schedule individually. See Chapter 9: The Black Box.

In general: Use every trick you know to make yourself start tackling Must + Now for even 15 minutes.

Then: Take walks, take breaks, and allow yourself not to think about anything for a while. Time your breaks, and get back to short sprints of work.

You've been out of focus-shape, and you're building up your focus-muscles. Forgive, forgive, forgive. It will take time.

How to tackle the Must + Can Wait list:

Allow yourself to forget these tasks for a few days. In order to calm your anxious brain and reassure it that you will deal with this stuff in good time, set a planning date with yourself on your calendar in the near future to schedule and break down these items (again, using the planning processes in Parts 1 and 2 of this book).

How to tackle the Would Like To + Can Wait list:

This is where things get really tough because it is probably where your dream project is sitting, and I know: It makes you feel like a loser not to put it on the schedule right now, today.

I'm telling you: You can do the big dream project, you can make it happen.

But get warmed up first. Get the panic-inducing Now stuff finished, or at least in progress, and practice the art of focus for a while before you move on to tackle the stuff that has no external deadlines or commitments. Make a date with yourself to plan your next project using this book and your Workbook. On that date, go back to Chapter 6 and set your feet on the path to finished.

Pro tip: the Now + Would Like To bucket should be empty.

How long restarting should take

There's no hard and fast equation here, but a general rule of thumb is that the longer you've been derailed, the longer it is likely to take to get started again and back on track. If you've only been out of it for a week, it'll likely take you a day or so to get in the groove. If it's been two months, and you're in a whole new environment, like I was after I moved back to the States, it'll take a lot longer. If you've never really had this down? Build up slowly, know this is really really hard, and forgive yourself when you fall short.

Try again, and forgive again. The biggest obstacle between you and full access to your creative productivity is that voice in your head that tells you this is all happening because you suck.

Conclusion

Designing a sustaining creative practice takes time, so go easy on yourself

You may have come to this book looking for tactical approaches to getting your self-generated creative work done. I hope you've found the tactics I've given you here helpful.

That said, you may be surprised, now that you've read the whole book, how much of creative productivity comes down to mindset. We set ourselves up for failure in so many ways, believing the stories we've been fed about how artists find inspiration, expecting levels of production that aren't reasonable, comparing how we work to stories we read about other artists who've been at this for years and years. Then when we inevitably fail to meet those standards, we feel like it's our job, our *duty*, to punish ourselves. Misery ensues.

Building a flexible, balanced, joyful, sustaining creative practice is a craft, not instinct.

It takes time and thought. The fact that you had to read this book and do a bunch of possibly annoying and certainly sometimes painful exercises to figure out your creative practice (and you still may not feel you're there) is completely normal and to be expected.

People think taking the time on introspection and developing a system to support their creative work will take away from the work. It's true that it takes time. In my experience, that time is a worthwhile investment. The time it takes to develop a creative practice is nothing in comparison to the time *wasted* on being scattered, procrastinating, and self-flagellating when you *don't* have a system.

If there's one thing I could wish for you above all, it would be that you give yourself a break.

My no. 1 productivity tip is:
Forgive yourself.

You *can* change who you are, and you don't have to be resigned to how things are working in your life. But you do have to take action, not just think about it, in order to change anything. You act into thinking; you don't think your way into acting. You can't change anything until you're actually in motion. And the only thing standing in the way of being in motion is inside your head. You deserve kind treatment from yourself. Start there.

If you enjoyed the book,

please leave consider leaving a review on Amazon.com!

Your review helps others discover

how to dive deep and swim.

http://bit.ly/growinggills

Made in the USA
Middletown, DE
29 December 2018